TALES OF NEVADA

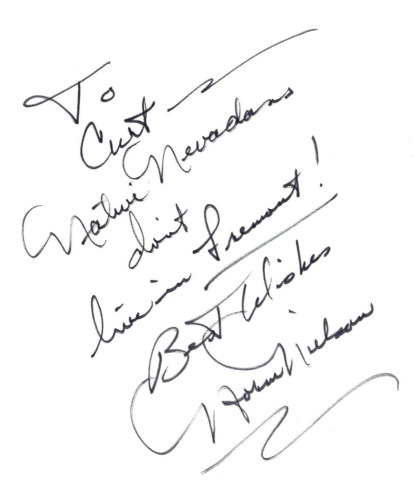

To Curt —
Native Nevadans
don't
live in Fremont!
Best Wishes
John Nielsen

TALES OF
NEVADA
by
NORM
NIELSON

Foreward by The Honorable Senator Richard Bryan

c 1989 by Norm Nielson

Typesetting and cover design by Art Associates, Reno, Nv.
Printed by Printing and Forms, Reno, NV
Binding by Reno Trade Bindery, Reno, NV

Published by:
    Tales of Nevada,
    2500 Parkway Drive
    Reno, Nv 89502

To Teri,
Happiness is a healthy outlook on life, a grateful spirit, a clear
conscience, and a heart full of love.
Thanks to you I have them all...

Contents

Introduction

Understanding Nevada's frontier heritage is important to understanding the Nevada of today. The enterprize, independence, and ingenuity of the early Nevada pioneers established the foundation upon which the Nevada we know today was built. Nevada's origins are unique. Its statehood was born of the civil war and the riches of the Comstock Lode. Nevada's first citizens—true explorers and fortune hunters—braved a hostile environment to seek riches and left countless tales of fortunes made and lost, of heroes and villains, of entrepreneurs and charlatans.

Despite the folklore surrounding the Old West, the Nevada story is about real people and their accomplishments. It is also a tale of endurance and adaptation as mines flourished and vanished, towns were built and abandoned, and the culture of the gold rush evolved into the modern west. Ghost towns and legends are the only legacy we have of Nevada's past.

Some of Nevada's earliest citizens, such as Mark Twain, became almost universally known. Others lived and died in obscurity. Fortunately, the lives of many early Nevadans are preserved in the stories that have been recorded for posterity.

Tales of Nevada provides a glimpse of Nevada's past. As can be seen from these stories, the state is rich in human experience, and proud of it's heritage. The pioneers left a legacy of strength and spirit, and like them Nevadans today are determined to preserve an independent spirit.

Through history, we can also review the future. As you enjoy the tales of Nevada's past, also look for messages for the Nevada yet to come.

United States Senator
Richard H. Bryan

Preface

Aren't you tired of people putting Nevada down?

I am. That's really the reason for this book.

Folks have always looked askance at us. We are known for gambling, divorce and prostitution and sadly, especially to folks east of the Mississippi, very little else.

It's our fault, of course. Nevadans have always prided themselves on their freedoms, hence the legalization of prostitution. We created, then carefully nurtured, the divorce industry. We did it simply for economic reasons; it was a stopgap against depression when the mines of the state petered out. And gambling? It's our state's largest industry. Though there has been a stigma attached to it since troops rolled the dice for the robe of Christ, true Nevadans know better. We know that gambling provides the lion's share of our state's revenues, monies for schools, roads, libraries and much, much more.

Still, much of the nation looks down its nose at Nevada...

"What do you people do BESIDES gamble?", they ask incredulously, as if we spend every waking moment in front of a slot machine.

"All you have out there is DESERT!", they exclaim, forgetting that the desert has a beauty all its own and that we have more lakes and mountains than you can shake a stick at.

"Nevada is the divorce capitol of the world...," they say. Unfortunately it does little good to tell them that most other states matched Nevada's liberal attitude more than 40 years ago. To tell them that in Nevada marriages outnumber divorces by more than 2-to-1 is a waste of breath.

There are a lot of misconceptions out there, and, frankly, I for one, am getting tired of it. This book, hopefully, will provide you with some interesting tidbits about the Silver State. Feel free to use them as ammunition to get the skeptics off your back.

Together, I hope we can convince our friends, relatives, and visitors that we're not really that much different than the rest of the nation. More independent, perhaps, but not different. We don't sport halos, of course, but we don't exactly wear horns either. Perhaps we can show them that even though we have in the past been known for divorce, prostitution and more, we are not, in this day and age, really going to go to hell in a handbasket.

So it is that I have put together this volume. I want to set the record straight. If just one person, yourself included, learns a little more about Nevada and the people who have made it what it is today, it will all be worth it...

Thanks so much for reading!

Norm Nielson
September 1989

Acknowledgements

Never drink wine with C.J.Hadley. Take my advice.

She started this whole thing, you know. There we were, she, the intrepid editor of Nevada Magazine and I, winging our way to Las Vegas for some conference or other. That's when it all began.

Despite her courageous efforts and 20-hour workdays, the Nevada legislature, in its infinite wisdom, was making noises about cutting off funding for the publication. "No problem.," I suggested, wine-fortified and anxious to come to the aid of a damsel in distress. "Why not give me some old issues of the Magazine and I'll create a radio version of some of the most interesting stories. We'll give them to radio stations around the state and that should get some attention."

Surprisingly enough, it worked. Within a few months, "Tales of Nevada!" had become a syndicated radio program and CJH had her funding, though it was due far more to her stamina and grit than my suggestion.

It took courage for those first radio stations to come on board. America was coming off a bloody and unpopular conflict in Vietnam and folks were saying that patriotism was dead. Even God Himself was dead, said some. With the country in an angry mood, who would be interested in a history program, much less a program about old Nevada?

But the managers of those radio stations were astute enough to recognize the true mood of the country back then. Somehow they knew that Americans, and, most particularly Nevadans, truly wanted to have their pride restored. They were right, and, thankfully for me, they stuck in there.

That was five years ago. It is now more than 1500 separate radio shows later and I am proud to say that KDWN in Las Vegas, KELK in Elko, KELK in Ely, KVLV in Fallon and KOH in Reno still carry the program today.

Tom Wilson, the veteran Reno ad man (and the man responsible for Nevada's first out-of-state advertising, the revolutionary 'Harold's Club or Bust!" campaign) gave me my love for this vast unpopulated state more than 20 years ago. He took a chance on the young writer, sending me off to write brochure copy about the far and desolate regions of the State. But he gave me so much more than a job. He took me out into the back country where he showed me tracks made by emigrant wagon trains back in the 1840's. "Be careful," he said, "this land scars easy." I have never forgotten.

There are a lot of people I will never forget as well, for their influence permeates this book. There is Marshall Fey, grandson of the inventor of the slot machine, who took me to task for not doing my homework and invited me to truly see Nevada for the first time. Bob and Lois Lyons, who opened their home to me when I first arrived, taught me not to take things too seriously.

Gene McKenna and Howard Doyle, of Doyle and McKenna Advertising, taught me that good writing, by necessity, requires caring. Lauri Vasquez, the man who designed the cover of this book and has donated countless hours to this town, taught me that good guys, even those intricately involved in the business community, don't really have to finish last. Fran Harvey, a very special lady, taught me that it is better to give than to receive. Kris Lohse, a brilliant artist/writer who spent a lot of hours editing these pages, taught me that the younger generation isn't so different after all. And Bob Laxalt, Nevada's premier writer, taught me that the gift of story telling is perhaps the most sacred gift of all.

But this book would not have been possible without the encouragement of Lorainne and Phil Olsson, publishers of Fun & Gaming Magazine, who, years ago, accepted my first column on Nevada history with the kind words "Don't make it dry. Write as people speak." To date, we have more than 200 columns in the "can," portions of which appear again here. There are many more yet to come.

But most of all, I am truly indebted to the hundreds of people who have told me their tales over the years. Unlike early on, when I had to pour painstakingly over the endless pile of research books, today most of my material comes from readers like you —from your old newspapers and diaries, from your old letters. I am honored, for it is not I, but YOU, who are the real historians of this state.

We are all a part of Nevada's heritage, of course; all of us are a part of our past. And thanks to a lot of very special people, I have slowly become a part of Nevada too.

It will take many more decades, of course, before I can call myself a native. But thanks to you, I'm getting mighty close...

THE RUSH WAS ON....!
-1-

Virginia City. Old time Nevadans are fond of saying that there wouldn't be a San Francisco without it. Yep, without the fabulous silver strike which shocked and awed the world, they say, the city by the Bay would have been nothing more than a muddy mission hanging from a wind-swept clift. Although old timers tend to exaggerate a bit, in this case they aren't far from wrong.

By the late 1860's Virginia City, Nevada boasted more than 30,000 souls. Not bad, really, when you consider that the place was little more than a barren rocky landscape in the shadow of Sun Mountain just a few short years before.

The town's bleak beginning was described by a Dr. Pierson in a letter to the Carson Tribune dated August, 1870:

"I visited the spot known as Virginia and found not a house, but two tents in the ground. One was owned by John L. Blackburn who died by an assassin's knife. I saw the first mine and formed an acquaintance with Mr.Comstock, the man whose name is perpetrated wherever mines are known throughout the world.

"I also met old Virginia for whom the place is named. On that day in June (1859), the writer saw $1900.00 in black gold valued at $11.00 an ounce washed out of the surface ground at the Ophir."

Two tents? That was it? From a region where a single mine was yielding an incredible $1900.00 a day? There should have been people swarming over the desolate Nevada hills like a swirling cloud of locust.

Of course, the hoards would come, but not for a few more months. What none of the men realized was that while the area did have impressive pockets of gold, it contained far richer deposits of silver. And that discovery would evolve almost by accident.

1

Most of the miners working the Gold Hill/Virginia City area were plagued by what most were calling "that infernal blue stuff". The substance appeared to be a completely worthless, soft, blue-tinted ore and it got in the way of "serious gold mining". As a result, most of the men just shoveled it angrily aside, usually pushing it unceremoniously down the mountainside where it accumulated in great ugly forgotten piles.

But one day a Carson rancher by the name of W.P.Morrison happened along. He was curious about the reported strikes in Gold Canyon and had stopped by for a personal inspection. Intrigued by the "blue stuff," he pocketed a sample with the intent on having it assayed. Morrison, however, promptly forgot about it.

It was several months before Morrison got around to having that famous sample analyzed. But eventually he happened across an assay office in Grass Valley, California. What he learned there would shock the world.

There was gold in the sample, alright, enough to enable assayer J.J.Ott to estimate that the yield would total almost $1600.00 a ton. But the real discovery was the fact that the sample also contained silver; in fact TWICE as much silver as gold! Incredible as it seemed, Ott was convinced that the "infernal blue stuff," the ore that was literally being thrown away by gold-hungry prospectors, would assay out at $4,971.00 a ton!

Virginia City reporter William Wright, known affectionately by his unique pen name of Dan DeQuille, picks up the story from there. "The excitement by no means abated when [the assayer] was informed by Mr. Morrison that there were tons and tons of the same stuff just lying in plain sight. It was agreed that the result of the assay should be kept a profound secret; meantime they would arrange to cross the Sierra and secure as much ground as possible..."

But keeping such a rich find a secret proved, quite naturally, impossible. By 9 o'clock the very next morning half the town of Grass Valley knew all about it. Even the local barrister, one Judge Walsh, had closed up shop, packed a mule with provisions, and was prepared to leave for the wilds of the Nevada Territory at the crack of dawn.

In a few more days hundreds of miners had left their diggings in California and were flocking over the mountains by whatever mode of transportation was available. Those without pack animals carried all they possessed on their backs and began the torturous trek on foot.

Wrote DeQuille, "The few hardy prospectors soon counted their neighbors by the thousands and found eager and excited newcomers jostling them on every hand, planting stakes under their very noses, running lines round and through their brush shanties as though they were Pah-Utes. The handful of old settlers found themselves strangers in their own land and their own dwellings in a single day."

Yep, the rush to Nevada was on; the cloud of frantic, hungry locust had arrived. Soon men were scrambling over the steep mountainside with reckless abandon. The land and the territory would never be the same again.

Sun Mountain (later to be named Mt. Davidson) would eventually yield one of the richest silver strikes in the nation's history. The tiny port of San Francisco would become the banking and investment capital of western America.

Just goes to show you. If you ever come across some "infernal blue stuff" out there in the desert, I would humbly suggest that you don't just throw it away...

NEVADA.
THE STATE OF DESERET
-2-

Salt Lake City, Utah is the world-wide headquarters of the Mormon Church, which, some say, is the wealthiest religious organization on the planet. But religion and finances aside, the Mormons had a most profound effect on what would become known as the State of Nevada. In fact, they tried to make it a state of their own. The State of Deseret...

History does not dispute the impact of the Mormon Church on the settlement of the Nevada territory. By 1850, the only people who had settled in the region were the Faithful. Everyone else had kept right on going to greener pastures along the Pacific Coast.

Having come west to escape religious persecution, the Mormons, from their headquarters by the Great Salt Lake, set out to colonize the remainder of the west. Joseph Smith and Brigham Young had both vowed that never again would the Mormons place their destiny in the hands of others.

It was 1847 when Mormon scout Jefferson Hunt made his way along the Old Spanish Trail which wound southwest across the desert from Salt Lake City into Alta California. He came across some deep, refreshing pools. He made a mental note that, despite the reports to the contrary, perhaps the arid desert could indeed provide leader Brigham Young with the tools for his plan for westward expansion.

The news was precisely what Young had wanted to hear. He had visualized a string of missions linking Salt Lake with the Pacific Coast. He had pictured ships unloading precious converts who would then make their way safely overland to the Mormon capitol.

Young sent 30 men under the command of William Bringhurst. A month later, with 40 ox-drawn wagons and 15 cows, they reached the pools which Hunt had first come upon. The route they

4

had traveled became known as the Mormon Trail and the mission they established would become Las Vegas.

The Mormons were phenomenally successful at colonization and staked claims throughout the territory. The cause was aided by the fact that the Federal Government, for the most part, was looking the other way.

They cultivated small farms and established the first mining claims. Although Mormon elders admitted their successful attempts at baptizing local Paiutes was more likely for food than for faith, they brought the first of the white man's religions to the natives. They mapped the best trade routes, even managing to obtain the first contract to carry the U.S. Mail. They established a prosperous lead mine near present-day Las Vegas.

They were equally successful in the north. In the valley south of what today is Carson City, they created Nevada's first permanent settlement, Mormon Station, later to become known as Genoa. By 1850 it was thriving. A man by the name of Robert Lyon described the outpost in an early diary.

"I arrived at the Station and lay resting for one day. I sold a good American horse to the man who kept the trading post for 30 pounds of flour and $15.00. Flour was $1.50 a pound so he allowed me $60.00 for my horse. There were two or three women at the place and I understand that they had settled there with the intention of remaining permanently".

"They had quite a band of fat cattle and cows which they had brought over from Salt Lake; some of the fattest cows I have ever seen hung suspended from the limbs of a big pine tree. They retailed the beef to hungry emigrants for 75 cents a pound and I have never eaten meat that tasted so sweet".

"There was one store where they kept for sale flour, beans, tea, coffee, sugar, shirts, etc. There was also a grocery where they sold whiskey, bread, cigars and tobacco. Mormon Station was indeed well established."

But a few settlements hardly constitute an empire. On March 18, 1849, Church elders assembled at a Salt Lake convention to create a territorial government. That government, it was determined, would preside over a brand new state, a state to be known as Deseret.

The 'state' was truly amazing in almost every sense of the word. For one thing, it was incredibly large, encompassing all the land which today is Utah, Nevada, Arizona and parts of Colorado, Oregon and Wyoming.

Portions of what today is California were also included, although there is no record of whether the Mexican government, true owners of the land, had been consulted on the matter. Areas which today are parts of Los Angeles and San Diego counties stretching west to Santa Monica, were staked off. It was an ambitious undertaking, to say the least, but Mormon leaders considered it vital to establishing a firm foothold in the west.

The U.S. Government, however, did not take kindly to the idea. There had already been a confrontation between Mormon leader Young and President James Buchanan, and when word reached Washington about the new 'state,' the United States Congress took immediate action. They weren't about to let a Church take over what amounted to almost one-quarter of the North American continent.

Six months later, on September 9, Congress created a 'state' of its own. It was called the Utah Territory and it was "bordered on the west by California, on the north by Oregon, on the east by the Rockies and on the south by the 37th parallel." The attempt at Mormon statehood was thwarted. Concerned about military reprisals, Young ordered his followers to return to Salt Lake and prepare for armed confrontation. The Mormon pioneers withdrew, leaving behind all they had so painstakingly established.

In a few more years, with the discovery of silver, another American President, Abraham Lincoln, would carve the State of Nevada from the Utah Territory. Residents of the region, now some 2,000 strong, would have a true identity for the first time.

But for some Mormon settlers, the idea of statehood was nothing new. As far as Mormon leaders were concerned, Nevada was already a state, the 'state' of Deseret.

"A great part of [the Great Basin] is absolutely new to geographical, botanical and geological science. We were evidently on the verge of the desert which had been reported to us. The appearance of the country is so forbidding that I was afraid to enter it."

—Capt. John Fremont—
Upon first seeing the region which
would eventually become Nevada in 1843

"It is such a fascinating land. For all it's hardship, I shall hate to leave it!"
—Capt. John Fremont
Upon leaving the territory the following year.

THE HANGING OF LUCKY BILL
-3-

They called him "Lucky Bill" Thorington, and indeed, for most of his life, he was.

Until, that is, they strung him up...

Bill Thorington was a native of New York State until 1848 when the family headed west. By 1853 he was on his own, a resident of the Carson Valley.

Even by frontier standards he was a giant of a man, topping the scales at more than 210 pounds and standing a towering 6 feet 1 inches. With his wavy jet-black hair and ever-present smile, he was a popular fellow, and although a gentile, he seemed to fit in well with the Mormon pioneers who had inhabited the region. It was rumored that he had even taken two wives, in Mormon fashion, though no one was certain. Nonetheless, he was looked upon as one of the "faithful" by the powerful Mormon Church.

His moniker, "Lucky Bill," was certainly accurate. At almost any form of gambling he seemed to have an incredible ability to always come out on top.

But he was not only lucky. He was generous as well.

One afternoon he happened to overhear a young couple at Mormon Station arguing loudly. The couple had come west with another man and a violent confrontation had taken place. The man had agreed to take the couple on the journey only if they would provide the food. The food had run out and the man refused to carry them any further.

Their plight intrigued Thorington. He engaged the wagoneer in a friendly game of thimblerig, a popular western variation of "find the pea", and, before long, he had won all of the man's money. After lecturing the hapless pioneer on the evils of gambling, Bill gave half of his winnings to the young couple and returned the

7

rest to the incredulous gambler with the understanding that he would "light out quick!" He then gave a cow to the bankrupt family and even hired a driver to see them on into California.

But such is the stuff of which legends are made. What happened next would bring Bill's winning streak to an abrupt end.

In the spring of 1858 an acquaintance of Bill's, William Edwards, had shot and killed a man in Merced County, California. The body of the murdered man was found tied in a sack which had been sunk in the Susan River. The citizens of the Honey Lake country took off in hot pursuit, but they were unable to catch up with Edwards.

As fate would have it, they came upon another man named Snow, and, believing him to be a party to the crime, they hung him without a trial. In the interim, Edwards, riding a stolen horse, far outdistanced the angry posse. He crossed the Sierra into Nevada, arriving a few days later at the ranch of Bill Thorington.

Knowing nothing of the murder, Thorington took pity on the fugitive. He agreed to put him up at the ranch for a few days, gave him some pocket money and even arranged to sell his horse. The horse 'buyers' turned out to be undercover agents investigating the murder. Thorington was taken into custody; Edwards escaped again.

The authorities questioned Bill Thorington about Edward's whereabouts. When they determined that Thorington couldn't — or wouldn't —tell them anything, they turned their attention to his young son Jerome. They told the boy that his father would surely hang unless Jerome told them where Edwards was hiding. The lad complied.

Edwards was captured, found guilty of murder and shipped off to California to be hanged. But instead of being released as he had been promised, Thorington was tried for murder as well.

Throughout the trial there was not a single bit of evidence that Bill had taken part in the murder. Indeed, he was nowhere near California at the time. Nonetheless, the townspeople found him guilty as charged.

Later accounts would hint that Thorington's friendship, his "love of Mormons," led to the verdict. For years there had been an uneasy truce between early Mormon pioneers who had settled the region and newcomers who had a profound dislike for any religion that "allowed one man to take a hundred wives."

No matter. On the 19th of June, 1858, Bill Thorington was placed on a wagon bed at the Clear Creek Ranch and a noose was jerked around his neck. The wagon was pulled from beneath him and he was dragged by the tightening rope from the vehicle. His body swung back and forth in the blustery Nevada wind until Bill Thorington finally choked to death.

So ended the luck of "Lucky Bill."

Did he really have two wives? He did, indeed. And later, accounts would show that his will had divided his belongings and property equally between them.

"Lucky Bill" Thorington was, it seems, generous even to the end...

STAKING A CLAIM ON
THE FABULOUS COMSTOCK
-4-

You might think that the first prospectors to hit the Comstock kept pretty close tabs on their property lines. Well, for the most part, that was true. But believe it or not, sometimes, if a miner wasn't particularly happy with his original claim, he simply went to the recorder's book and changed it!

When you think back to the days when picks and shovels were flying recklessly about, one can't help but picture all that silver lying deep below ground. There it was, resting quietly beneath the ever-changing shadow of Mount Davidson —millions of dollars worth of glittering quartz just waiting for someone with curiosity to come along.
And along they came. By the thousands. The earliest arrivals were uneducated. Some could not read, most could not write and it was painfully evident in the way the first records of the earliest claims were kept.
Charged with that somewhat dubious responsibility was Virginia City's first County Recorder, one V.A. Houseworth, a part-time blacksmith. If a miner wished to stake his claim, he simply paid a visit to Houseworth, plunked down the customary $3.00 and wrote his property description in the tattered book.
One of the earliest entries was penned by two Irishmen, Pat McLaughlin and Peter O'Riley, the men generally credited with discovering the original mother lode:
"Notice. We, the undersigned, claim 600 feet of this quartz vein, commencing with the south end of Finney and Company [Author's note: James Finney, also known as Ol' Virginny, along with the unscrupulous Henry Comstock, was another of the original discoverers of what would become known as the Comstock Lode] and running south 600 feet and two chains." Notice there

is no mention of even the approximate location of Finney and Co., a common problem at the time.

To further complicate matters, the two men also penned this rather indescriptive notation: "We, the undersigned, claim this spring and stream for mining purposes." Again, no mention of what stream or even where it might be found.

How about this confusing little ditty? "We claim 2,000 feet of this quartz lead, ledge, lode or vein, beginning at the stake and running north." Where was this mysterious stake? No one really knew.

Naturally this situation caused more than a few problems and a considerable number of heated arguments were the inevitable result. While the miners were feverishly toiling with shovel and pick, fledgling attorneys (many without benefit of either schooling or credentials) were getting rich trying to decide just 'who' actually owned 'what'. Adding insult to injury, more than a few of the legal profession were not above giving the scales of justice a little tip from time to time.

One particular dispute involved two miners who claimed that each was the rightful owner of a small parcel that jutted out from an old tree stump. Each claimed that the stump was the pivotal point on which his claim was based and each claimed identical ownership.

The feud came to a head in open court when one of the miners produced several "witnesses" who swore that they could identify the elusive aforementioned stump. Court was promptly adjourned and the participants agreed to meet at first light the following morning.

But upon arriving at the site, the jury was astounded. The stump was gone. It had simply disappeared. Unbeknownst to the judge and his hapless jury, during the night the attorney for the defense had been burning the midnight oil. He had hired some workmen who had dug up the stump, filled in the hole and obliterated any trace of its previous existence. The whole matter was dropped for lack of "a suitable stump" and the defense attorney earned himself an extremely healthy fee.

Early record keeping on the Comstock certainly left a lot to be desired. But even if the records themselves were sloppily kept, the confidentiality of the "official" recorder's book was a problem even more serious.

Lacking a permanent office from which to conduct business, Recorder Houseworth, for convenience sake, kept his record book behind the bar at a local saloon. That's right, behind the bar! Anyone who wished to consult the now-forlorn but hallowed journal had only to reach over the weathered plank and help himself, no questions asked.

Naturally this precarious situation created more than a few problems of its own. By the time the journal was safely locked up in the newly-constructed recorder's office, numerous claims — some of which would eventually result in finds worth millions — had been scratched out and hastily re-entered. Entire pages had been torn away.

For the most part however, the majority of the miners were too busy digging to give all this hanky-panky much serious thought. It was a case of "dig now" and worry about the doggone legalities later. Such goings-on were tolerated on the slopes of the Mountain in those early days and perhaps the men wouldn't have had it any other way.

In any event, it mattered little to McLaughlin and O'Riley. Regardless of the ambiguity of their recorded claims, together they went on to amass a small fortune, though they would lose it again just as rapidly.

On the Comstock, it seems, a man's word was infinitely more valuable than a few scribbled lines in anyone's old book...

"I arrived at the Station and lay resting for one day. I sold a good American horse to the man who kept the trading post for 30 pounds of flour and $15.00. The flour was $1.50 a pound so he allowed me $60.00 for my horse.

"There were two or three women at the place and I understood that they had settled there with the impression of remaining permanently. They had quite a band of cattle they had brought over from Salt Lake; some of the fattest cows I have ever seen hung suspended from the limbs of a big pine tree. They retailed the beef to hungry emigrants for 75 cents a pound. I have never since eaten beef that tasted so sweet.

—Pioneer Robert Lyon—
Describing Mormon Station, Nevada's
first permanent settlement in 1850

TERROR ON THE FRONTIER
-5-

It was 1864.

Nevada's statehood seemed imminent. Adding to the feeling of excitement, the mines of Virginia City were spewing out untold wealth and thousands of men and more than a few women were flocking to Nevada in hopes of striking it rich.

But if the mood of the population was one of jubilant anticipation, it was also one of nervous forboding. There were two major forces that could bring an end to the good life and instant wealth that lay in the shadow of Mount Davidson. One was the Civil War; the other was marauding Indians.

For months rumors had been circulating about a possible raid by Confederate forces on the mines of Virginia. The South was in the choking grip of a Union blockade. The Confederacy was in desperate need of supplies or, at the very least, enough money to entice daring blockade runners. The army of the South looked covetously at the riches of Nevada.

With little or no substantiation, local newspapers fanned the flames. Wrote the Virginia City Union, "The authorities of the Territory have been warned to look out for a gang of thieves and Secessionists who are now among us, or design coming here for the purpose of burning and plundering Virginia City and Carson City to as great an extent as possible. Secessionists are now flooding to us altogether too fast, by land and sea, and it behooves all loyal citizens to keep a lookout for them."

The territory was decidedly uneasy. Many, including the editors of the Gold Hill News, thought that the Confederacy had devised a master plan to infiltrate the Comstock. "That suspicious bands are today hidden away in the unfrequented fastness of the mountains and plains east of here is established beyond a doubt. It will be seen, therefore, that the quiet organization of our home guard and its arming has been a wise and necessary precaution. Citizens who have been surprised at the appearance of so many of our townsmen armed and equipped as the law directs will now perceive the object."

But a more pressing threat was lurking in Nevada.

"A savage attack was made by a large body of Indians on five American miners a few days ago. The miners were camped at a spring near a point of rocks when they found themselves surrounded. All the miners were wounded in the first attack; one, however, not so severely as the others. He assisted his companions to the shelter of the rocks where they employed themselves in loading the guns and pistols which he fired at the savages with such deadly effect that over 20 of them lay dead when the Indians gave up the attack. They retired, carrying off their dead, and the wounded men finally reached a place of safety. One of them, S. Herring, died of his wounds."

Terror spread through the mining camps. Almost daily new reports began to appear. "There is every possibility that we are on the eve of an Indian war on an extensive scale throughout the entire West," wrote the Reese River Reveille. "The Indians are hourly committing new depredations. Five or six hundred miles west of St. Joseph, 11 stations of the Overland Mail have been destroyed and 35 station keepers murdered. The Overland Mail has been suspended for the present and our only communication with the East will be by California steamers."

Although the 'depredations' actually took place hundreds of miles from Nevada, their effects were immediate. Nevadans, even in the most metropolitan of mining camps, were now almost completely isolated from news from the eastern seaboard, forced to wait many months while the mail and eastern newspapers made their tortureous route by clipper and steamship around Cape Horn.

The Indian attacks came closer, to the very outskirts of Austin. "There arrived today by way of Salt Lake, a wagon train presenting a terribly battered appearance. It reports one of the most hard-fought crossings of which we have heard. The train left St. Joseph with 30 wagons but lost 11 of them and nearly half its people in battles with the Indians.

"Making its situation doubly desperate," the paper continued, "its wagon master and guide were both killed, leaving nobody who

1 4

had ever made the trip before.

With word from the east cut off, Westerners relied on their own to keep them posted of new developments. Wrote the Virginia City Union, "We learn from Gridley, the famous Sanitary Flour Sack Man, that a telegraph operator reached Austin who stated that the Indians are consolidating their forces on the plains." (Author's Note: Reuell Gridley was the region's most famous citizen, having toured the mining camps auctioning off a sack of flour, proceeds of which went to the Sanitary Commission, forerunner of the modern Red Cross.) "General Connor sends word for the people to be prepared for a big Indian fight. There seems to be a combination of Indian tribes in this campaign."

Fear raced headlong across the Comstock. "A wagon train arriving from Salt Lake reports it was attacked by Indians 100 miles west of Fort Laramie and seven of its members, including one woman, were killed in the battle. Several more were wounded. Two women and two children were captured. One of the women is believed to have escaped but the two children were later found murdered and scalped.

But surprisingly enough, the furor in the Territory began to subside almost as quickly as it had appeared. As the year 1864 drew to a close, most residents, flushed with a new series of silver strikes, no longer saw a rebel soldier or an Indian lurking behind every rock and tree.

On October 31st, President Lincoln welcomed Nevada into the Union and worries about a Confederate raid on the Comstock dwindled. The war's end followed shortly, laying permanently to rest any doubts. The state entered a new and astounding era of prosperity.

As for the Indian issue, local residents slowly began to realize that most of Nevada's Indians were actually quite peaceful. In fact, on November 19, Austin's newspaper noted sadly, "A number of Shoshone of the female persuasion were busily engaged yesterday gathering sage brush seeds in the upper portion of the city. Pine nuts are very scarce this year and it behooves the squaws to secure a substitute. They can gather about a gallon of sage brush seeds each per day."

Then, as if in resignation that the days of hostility were finally coming to an end, the editor added, "They are doing their best, but it seems possible that we are going to have to give them some help before the winter is over...”

The days and nights of terror on the frontier had ended.

THE LONGEST TELEGRAM IN HISTORY
-6-

I know that compared to most, Nevada's a pretty young state. It's just that I'm getting tired of hearing about it —how, compared to other states, we're just young whippersnappers who have yet to grow up. Wherever I go I always run into someone from back east and when they learn that I'm from Nevada they look at me as if I was diseased.

There's a reason, of course. When your state is only 125 years old, some people have a tendency to look down their blue-blooded noses at you. Eastern residents are notorious. On the eastern seaboard folks can trace their ancestry back, not generations, but many hundreds of years and they can get downright fanatical about it. They are fond of saying how some distant relative braved the ocean blue and gallantly stepped ashore at Plymouth Rock or how their great-great-great-great granddaddy white-washed Monticello for "Ol' Tom" Jefferson. Even relative newcomers —those whose ancestors braved the horrors of Ellis Island in the early 1900's are becoming braggarts. Lee Iacocca has become a regular master at it.

I'm not really complaining about the fact that a lot of people are downright proud of their ancestry. I am, too. In fact, damn proud. But when we're talking about Nevada, I feel a little sorry for those of us who live here —comparatively speaking, of course. We've only been poking around in the Territory for about 140 years (If you don't count John Fremont's travels) and that doesn't seem quite long enough to establish a good track record.

Nonetheless, we've a lot to be proud of in our short history. In fact, if it weren't for Nevada, there probably wouldn't be a United States as we know it today. So if you're looking for something to say the next time Aunt Martha from Massachusetts starts bragging about the color of her blood, let her have it:

It was back in 1864. Seems a tall, gangly fella by the name of Lincoln was running for a second term as President of the United States and it was tough going. You see Lincoln was backing something called the 13th Amendment to the Constitution, an act to abolish slavery. The Amendment made Lincoln very popular north of the Mason-Dixon line but to Southerners, he was the devil incarnate.

Abe Lincoln found himself sitting on a fence with supporters and opponents almost equally divided. To convince a southern state to change its allegiance was no longer a possibility. The Civil War had convinced him of that. Bullets were still flying, men were still dying. Appomattox was still a long way off.

So Lincoln hit upon another idea. If he couldn't win another state, perhaps he could create a brand new one. It was then that he set his sights on the Nevada Territory.

Nevada was inviting for several reasons. Out here we had a little silver strike going on. Called the Comstock Lode, it was rumored to be the richest find in world history. While few in Nevada were paying much attention to the War Between the States, most still had northern sympathies. Lincoln reasoned, and rightly, that should statehood be possible, most residents would vote in favor of his critical amendment. Besides, if Nevada joined up, the Union would have a crack at that great big mountain of silver. For the financially strapped Union and its desperate President, Nevada was an inviting package —votes and money all at the same time.

So a campaign for statehood was launched. Though the region was sparsely populated at the time, Lincoln politely looked the other way as thousands of transient miners and prospectors —most of whom had been in the area just a few short months, suddenly became "outstanding citizens of a most progressive state!"

There were fiery speeches from Carson City streetcorners, flags and banners fluttered along the Comstock. With relatively little urging, Nevadans voted to join the United States of America.

But in order to meet the legal requirements, the Constitution of the new state had to be delivered to Washington D.C. in person. The problem was acute. The Pony Express was just an idea at the time and the fastest way for mail to traverse the country was by ship to San Francisco and then by horseback over the mountains, a journey that took at times more than 2 months.

Eventually it was decided to send Nevada's Constitution, word by word, by telegraph to Chicago. There it would be written down once again in longhand and taken overland to Washington. If the telegraph lines were operating...

It was a monumental undertaking and the result was the longest telegram in history. It took a fledgling telegrapher, one Frank Bell (cousin of Alexander Graham Bell), more than 12 hours just to tap it out. It cost almost $4,000.00 to send!

But it did the trick. Lincoln won re-election, Nevada was shortly ushered into the Union, the 13th Amendment was passed and soon the American Civil War came to its end. Perhaps it would never have happened had it not been for a very rich new state with a very tiny population.

So the next time your eastern friends begin harping at you about Nevada, tell 'em to go stuff it. We're every bit as important to the history of this country as any other state, perhaps more so. And we're damned proud of it.

Incidentally, the telegrapher, Frank Bell, went on to become one of our first Governors. There is absolutely no truth to the rumor that he was the first and the last person to read our State Constitution in its entirety...

"Deep sand which continued for 14 miles. I saw 200 wagons [abandoned] in one half mile and dead animals so thick you could step from one to another...

—Early Pioneer George Reed—
1850
Fearful Crossing

A FLEDGLING CAPITOL...

-7-

The book is a heavy one.

It's the 1881 "History of Nevada", and it's a toughy. It's almost 700 pages long and it's printed in such small type that my eyes tire even after a few moments. But though it's inaccurate at times, when you want to get a good initial working knowledge of early Nevada, this volume is definitely the place to turn.

Some people, of course, can't stand history. In every school room in the country you can still hear the age-old complaint, "Gosh, why do we have to learn all this OLD stuff???"

In some respects you can't blame the young for feeling as they do. After all, to them, history is old hat; it's dead, dead and gone. The future is infinitely more exciting and it should be. But myself, I read history books like a football coach whose team is bound for the Super Bowl —to see where we've been and what we've become —and why.

Above all, I peruse the old history books to make sure that we don't make more than just a few of the same old mistakes again. It's a policy I heartily recommend to anyone considering running for public office. In fact, it should be mandatory.

Today, for example, Carson City, our capitol, is enjoying a new and exciting period of growth. As is my habit before writing about Carson today, I pulled out the trusty 1881 history to see what it was like "way back when".

Here's just a sample: In 1860 Carson had but one school teacher and one jeweler. There were two tinners (tin smiths to the uninitiated), 5 lawyers, doctors and painters. There were 7 upholsterers, 20 carpenters, 46 teamsters and blacksmiths. Number of bookmakers: 6. Number of barbers: ditto.

The city boasted 2 boarding houses, 3 restaurants, 7 hotels, 10 saloons and 32 other assorted shops and stores. And incidentally, the town had not one, but 6 breweries.

Wages? They certainly left a lot to be desired. A farmhand made $3.00 a day (50 cents more if you didn't have to feed him). Carpenters made a good deal more —$7.00 a day, but the work was sporadic, dependent upon the amount of lumber available, which was little, especially during the winter months. 'Female help' was paid $40.00 a month with food and lodging generously thrown in.

And up in the mines of Virginia City and nearby Gold Hill, despite the abundance of gold and silver, things weren't really that much better. Although Nevada's underground work force was among the highest paid in the world (wages in Nevada rose to as much as $5.00 daily; European miners made less than $1.00), living expenses took a heavy toll. The cost of a room, $4.00 a day with bathing extra, soon ate up most of the salaries of even the thriftiest of Irish workmen. A stay at a Carson City boarding house, such as the kind frequented by John Wayne in his final movie "The Shootist", set you back $20.00 in hard earned dollars each week.

And although the residents of Carson were undoubtedly a hearty bunch, they were, like most residents of frontier towns, highly susceptible to illness. In 1859, John Calvin, 29, Sandra Perkins, 16, and her 4 year old sister Louisa all died of typhoid. Thomas Owsley, age 2, died of deadly cholera. Forty year old Mary Jones died of some mysterious ailment known only as "congestion of the brain", while William Edwards, a 51 year old farmer, died of something called "mountain fever". And those were only the deaths recorded.

But such was life in Carson City back in 1860, four years before Nevada's statehood. As the stats show, there was tremendous growth but little permanency. Disease was commonplace; physicians sadly in short supply.

And for Carson to remain the capitol city at all was difficult. In fact, there were a lot of folks around that thought the capitol should be moved a lot closer to the action. Most of the hustle and bustle was taking place up on the nearby Comstock Lode and a lot of people (just like present-day Las Vegas lawmakers who still grumble about it) weren't too happy about trekking up and down the mountain every time they needed to conduct a little business in the hallowed halls of government.

In the beginning Carson had offered to host the Territorial legislature for free and had provided meeting halls and the like all at no cost. But as the city grew, it was suggested that the good folks of Ormsby County start charging the government for services rendered. The amount decided upon was no small fee. Carson City demanded $4500 for each legislative session.

Quite naturally this unexpected and dramatic increase led some people to start looking around for a new location. The move to find a new site for an entirely new capitol rapidly gained momentum. In January of 1864, just a few scant months before statehood, a group of Comstock businessmen put up a substantial amount of money and actually laid out a new townsite on the flats south of Gold Hill. They called it, in typical patriotic fashion, American City. Then, to sweeten the pot, they offered the legislature the then-fabulous sum of $50,000 to move.

But the idea turned out to be nothing more than a tempest in a teapot. Despite the head-turning offer, most members of the legislature preferred the good life in the Carson Valley to the hardships of living "up on the mountain" where the snows drifted to 8 feet or more and the wind howled constantly. Carson City was the capitol and Carson City it remained.

So today, the key to consistent but controlled growth can still be found in our history books. Today, as we look at the new growth that is taking place in our number one city we must look carefully —at the water and the traffic problems, at the need for new housing and new industry.

But first, it is perhaps helpful to reflect upon how and how much the city has grown in 125 years. As we plan for the future, those old history books, despite what your restless and doubting youngster might say, just might come in handy...

THE DAY THE
PRESIDENT CAME TO TOWN...
-8-

Ever notice that there's never a President around when you need one? Every night, there he is on the evening news speaking to us from somewhere —the Oval Office, a factory in Detroit, a barnyard in Iowa, a tenement in New York. In fact, he's everywhere but here.

We have problems, don't we? Problems with our highways, our water, our pollution? To make matters worse, some folks in Washington are still trying to bury their nuclear garbage out here.

If we have just as many legitimate troubles as the rest of the nation, where the hell is he (or she)? Unfortunately —depending of course upon your point of view —hardly ever do you see a real, live, honest-to-goodness American President out here in the Silver State.

'Course, that wasn't always the case. As a matter of fact, we were downright popular with presidents until the ore ran out.

Abe Lincoln, he liked us. He liked us a lot. There was a catch, of course. Ol' Abe had his hands full with a raging Civil War and his army of the Potomac was rapidly running out of money. Abe wanted to be re-elected. In addition, he wanted to pass an anti-slavery amendment and to do it, he needed to create an entirely new state. Nevada could help him out with both of his problems.

We had silver mines cranking out hundreds of thousands of dollars a day. We also had, though just barely, enough residents to qualify for statehood. Yep, Abe Lincoln liked us a lot.

U.S. Grant liked us too. When the war was over and things calmed down a bit, he stopped by to examine the silver mines first hand, resplendent in his old blue uniform. You can still see photos of him as he posed with Nevada miners and mine owners at the mouth of a shaft, ever-present cigar in hand, smiling as all politicians have smiled since the dawn of time. You can just imagine him thinking, "Boy, with all this silver lying around, who needs to mess with politics!"

Back in 1880 Rutherford B. Hayes also came calling. The Gold Hill News gushed, "This morning bunting was run up on all the hoisting works, on public buildings and most of the private houses and business places showed flags in more or less profusion."

"When the train neared town," the paper continued, "the scream of the whistles was noisy and musical. The flag on top of Mount Davidson was supplemented by that from the flagstaff of the Homestead (mine), beneath which and guarded by banners was a strip of canvas on which were the words, 'Welcome to President Hayes'."

"As the procession neared the ridge of the Divide, all the steam whistles along the northern part of the Lode chimed in, raising a roar that was almost deafening, and above it rose the boom of cannons!"

From the balcony of the International Hotel, Hayes spoke admiringly of the "remarkable engineering skills that had been brought about by the search for treasure," and then he warned the miners that they should take care of themselves, for "Good health is a treasure beyond all price."

It was a typical speech. But Hayes wasn't fooling anyone. Most people knew that all he really cared about was making sure that Nevada silver continued to flow and that its citizens continued to vote. That vote, though small, carried a lot of weight in eastern industrial circles. Nevada packed a whallop with east-coast and European bankers as well.

But that was yesterday.

Today the great mines of Nevada legend have long since petered out and consequently the days when Presidents really cared about the state are over.

In more recent times, most Presidents actually have looked the other way. While Bobby Kennedy was sniffing about the darkened halls of the Teamster's Union, his brother John was careful to place as many miles as possible between himself and the "notorious" image of the State of Nevada. Aside from an occasional conversation with Howard Hughes, Dick Nixon gave us a wide birth too. Johnson, Ford and Carter likewise.

Did I forget Ronald Reagan? Nope. I fully realize that he came here more times than almost all the other Presidents combined.

But I don't think Ron counts, and not just because he liked Paul Laxalt either.

I don't think he counts because he got one of his big breaks out here. You see, he once had a nightclub act at the Last Frontier in Las Vegas. He was sharing the bill with the Continentals and the Dancing Adorabelles (Boy, I bet they were something!). And, just as during his Presidency, the people loved him and the critics hated him. Wrote one Las Vegas reviewer, "Ron Reagan demonstrates the kind of humor that killed vaudeville!".

Yep, it's a shame there's never a President around when you need one. Of course, I guess it's understandable. After all, we have only a couple of electoral votes —hardly enough to get very excited about. And besides, the Feds already own more than 85% of the state anyway, so why should they care?

But if you're looking for a good nightclub act, now THAT'S another story...

"About midnight our neighbor approached our campfire and told us his only child had just died and he had come to solicit aid to bury it. We promised that in the morning his wants would be attended to.

"We had an empty cracker box which we made answer for a coffin, dug a grave in the middle of the road and deposited the dead child therein. The sun had just risen and was a spectator to that mother's grief as she turned slowly but sadly away from that little grave to pursue the long journey before her.

"We filled the grave with stones and dirt, and when we rolled out we drove over it. Perhaps we had cheated the wolf by so doing —perhaps not.

—Early pioneer John Clark—
1852
Fearful Crossing

THE $2,000 UNDIES
-9-

When a new town began to take root in Nevada, the first permanent structure was usually the saloon. As the town began to prosper and more and more buildings sprung up, the saloon in turn expanded, becoming first a place to eat, later a place to rent a moldy cot in the event you were doing more than just passing through.

The frontier saloon was totally unique to the American scene. It was at times a meeting hall, a courtroom, a place for politicians and preachers to hold forth. In short, it was the hub of virtually all important activity. In fact, the future success of any early boomtown could be measured quite accurately by the price of its libations. Wrote Comstock reporter Alf Doten, "When the price of drinks reaches two bits, you know you're on a roll!"

Despite what you've seen on television or in the movies, more than a few of the early saloon keepers were women, surprisingly enough. They may have been looked down upon if they worked in such a place, but if they were on the other side of the plank — if they owned the joint —it was quite another matter. It meant that, as "owner," a woman was automatically a citizen of more than a little wealth and respect.

Such a person was Mrs. Anna Harvey, at least for a time back in 1882. Austin's answer to Gunsmoke's Miss Kitty, Harvey ran a tidy little saloon during the early boom period. But when the mines inevitably began their agonizingly slow decline, her watering hole did likewise. True to the equation, the price of drinks went down and Harvey's debts began to pile up.

She ultimately decided that the only sure way out of the impending predicament was to skip town. After all, she reasoned, with business on the skids and a mountain of bills facing her, the best thing to do was simply pull up stakes and try someplace else.

With her teenage daughter in tow, Mrs. Harvey began to pack her bags.

But word travels fast, especially in a small town. Soon the rumors of her sudden departure reached the ears of one Gus Bauer, an Austin brewer, and Bauer had more than a passing interest in Mrs. Harvey. You see, she owed him the whopping sum of $11.00, roughly the price of two kegs of his popular homemade beer. Being the fastidious businessman that he was, Gus Bauer decided to confront Mrs. Harvey about the debt personally.

He arrived at her home. It was deserted. Immediately, he headed for the railway station and there, just as he had suspected, he found Harvey and her daughter waiting to board the afternoon train.

Without missing a beat, Bauer headed for the Sheriff's office and returned within minutes with a deputy. Seeing the two men approaching, mother and daughter beat a hasty retreat into a back room of the station. When the men burst through the door they found the good Mrs. Harvey, lo and behold, undressing!

Startled, and more than a little sheepish, the men withdrew, but not for long. Realizing that Mrs. Harvey might be pulling a ruse, the deputy began pounding on the door. After several minutes the men reentered to find Harvey had slipped off her bloomers and was in the process of hiding them in a dusty corner.

The deputy gingerly bent down to pick them up.

To his surprise, he found that it was not the flimsy silken nether garment he had been expecting. In fact, the bloomers were downright heavy.

And for good reason. Closer examination revealed that Mrs. Harvey had hidden a small fortune in $20.00 gold pieces, each ingeniously sewn into the lining of her underwear. In the waistband she had placed two in a row and carefully quilted them into the material. There was a single row of coins encircling each leg hole. Two side pockets had been fashioned and more gold hidden there as well.

In all, Mrs. Anna Harvey, the "poor" saloon keeper, had been about to make off with more than $2,000 carefully concealed in her simple little undergarment. The Reese River Reveille wrote with more than a touch of humor, "It must have been an exceedingly awkward and heavy load for any woman to carry. It was a wonder she could even walk!"

Mrs. Harvey did not pass "go." She went directly to jail. Not only was she forced to pay the $11.00 owed to brewer Bauer who had started the whole thing, but her subsequent trial caught the attention of the town's dedicated tax collector. This most distinguished gentleman decided to re-examine the books of her now-defunct saloon. He soon discovered that Mrs. Harvey owed more to the county than to the tenacious brewer. He promptly approached the court, hand extended, palm up. Mrs. Harvey's "savings" were confiscated.

So ended one of the most bizarre escape attempts in the history of Nevada. The incident created such a stir that for a time the infamous underwear was kept on display at the Austin jail so that the curious could stop by and see for themselves the fine example of crafty seamstressing.

And the brewer, Mr. Bauer? He became quite a celebrity. Much to his obvious delight, he became known far and wide as the man who had "sniffed out and tracked" the notorious lady in the $2,000 underwear.

JUSTICE
AT THE END OF A ROPE
-10-

No one in Virginia City was ever quite sure what had started it all.

Bill Smith was a popular fellah, a miner, -genial, apparently well-liked by all. But on the evening of March 5, 1871, he was found lying on his back in the doorway of the International Saloon, a bullet hole through his left eye. His blood and brains were slowly staining the weathered planks of the stoop.

The man who had pulled the fatal trigger was Arthur Perkins, a 24-year old New Yorker who had most recently been employed tinkling the ivories at Scott's Dancehall. Although Perkins was known as a "sport" and a "rounder", there seemed to be no reason at all for the gruesome murder. Smith had talked publicly about his support of Germany, then engaged in a war in Europe and Perkins was a well-known German baiter. But was that enough to kill a man in cold blood?

No matter. Smith was dead and the folks on the Comstock didn't take too kindly to it.

Perkins was immediately arrested. There was little doubt that he had been involved. Numerous eye witnesses had come forward. A crowd of more than 300 gathered in the street on the day of his arrest, prepared to take him off to the nearest hanging tree, but deputies armed with shotguns managed to disperse the angry crowd and spirit the killer off to the relative safety of the new jail. Arthur Perkins wouldn't be there long...

Just after midnight, volunteer firefighter Sam Wycknham, the steward of Young America Engine Company No.1, was asleep in the engine house. Suddenly he was awakened by a masked man, given a pistol and rudely shoved up into the belfry. "If anyone shows up, ring the alarm bell," he was told. "Then shoot him."

Meanwhile, Sheriff Atkinson and Undersheriff Stoner were also asleep, both rolled up on cots in their room at the rear of the Sheriff's Office. They were awakened by a vicious pounding on the door and when they rose to investigate, a dozen armed and masked men pushed their way inside and held the startled officers at gunpoint. Soon the strangers were joined by two dozen others. When the Sheriff refused to surrender the cell keys, the men systematically ransacked the office.

After the hasty search the keys to the jail cell were finally located and while several of the men held the lawmen at bay, the remainder broke into the cell of the helpless Arthur Perkins.

"We've come for you. Get dressed!" was the command.

Perkins pleaded with them, claiming that he had never intended to kill Smith, that "It was an accident." Cowering in fright, he struggled helplessly to pull on his boots. "Never mind 'em," he was told. "You won't be needing them." Barefoot, Arthur Perkins was hauled out into the cold of the endless Nevada night.

The jail had been totally surrounded, completely isolated from the rest of the city. There was a party of some 40 vigilantes in front, patrolling B Street. Curious passersby were told to "go about your business!" and if they hesitated, however slightly, menacing sixguns appeared. On A Street, at the rear of the jail, similar confrontations were taking place.

Silently, but making no attempt to conceal themselves, the vigilantes formed a circle around the terrified Perkins and moved along C Street to Sutton Avenue. From there they turned and climbed the rise to the Ophir Mine where a small building stood over the opening to one of the main shafts. A beam, some 12 feet from the ground, projected from the building front and beneath it. The tracks of the ore carts gleamed dully in the cold moonlight.

A piece of board was thrown across the tracks and Perkins was hoisted upon it. A rope was thrown over the beam and roughly tightened around his trembling neck.

Resigned to his fate, Perkins made a desperate attempt to help the hangman. As the board was pulled from beneath him, the doomed man leaped into the air and came crashing down. But his frantic efforts to greet death quickly were to no avail. His neck didn't break. Arthur Perkins was left to strangle slowly in the angry wind.

At 4 a.m. the body was discovered where the vigilantes had left it, suspended from the beam, still swinging eerily, grotesquely above

i. His hands and feet were still tied and a towel was still in place across the sightless eyes.

But there was no mystery to what had taken place. To the left lapel of his coat was a small placard on which was scrawled the following: "Arthur Perkins - Committee No. 601."

It was over.

The 601, of course, was the well-known Committee of Vigilance, an organization which, for a time, had a chapter in almost every town across the state. But that mattered little to Arthur Perkins.

The verdict of the coroner's jury was simple and to the point. Wrote the foreman, "Arthur Perkins, born at sea, aged 24 years, has come to his death on the 25th day of March, 1871, from strangulation by hands unknown..."

"Really I do not blame them for stealing anything to eat, for there is not anything at all in this country for them to eat except mesquite and lizards. The wolves here are as thin as a greyhound that has had nothing to eat for two months...

—Mormon pioneer John Steele—
1856
He was referring to Indian thievery at a new settlement which would become known as Las Vegas.

A HONEYBEE STARTED IT ALL...
-11-

Got to talking with a couple of old timers the other day. As those who are interested in the past are wont to do, we were reminiscing about the twists of fate that have shaped our history, about how fact is oft-times much stranger than fiction.

Phillip Deidesheimer was a case in point. A young German engineer, Deidesheimer had come to America to make his fortune and made instead what was perhaps the single most important contribution to Nevada's history.

Born in 1832, Deidesheimer had graduated from the prestigious Freiberg School of Mines, Europe's premier mining institute. Freiberg had produced the most renowned geologist of the time, Baron Von Richtoven, and offered the finest schooling available. But Europe was in turmoil. Faced with hunger, plague and revolution, entire families were emigrating to America, the so-called "Land of Opportunity."

Deidesheimer arrived in San Francisco by clipper ship in 1851 and soon took up residence in Hangtown (now Placerville, California) in the heart of the gold rush country.

At the time, the most common method of unearthing California gold was placer mining, a process of scraping away layers of earth either by hand or with the help of huge water cannons. Though the most effective method known in America at the time, placering provided little challenge to the inquisitive young engineer. And soon, the fields of gold began to disappear.

But in Virginia City, Nevada, things were just getting started. Just a few short years before a fabulous underground river of silver ore had been discovered and operations were feverishly underway. Wild rumors were circulating about "untold riches" and "silver for the taking." Another strike was on and miners by the thousands crossed over the Sierra from California. They would be shocked by what they discovered.

The river of silver lay deep underground. In some places it measured 40 feet wide, in others more than 200 feet across. It wound its way snakelike through the dark underbelly of Mount Davidson. Problem was: how to get to it. You see, rich as it was, much of it was over a quarter of a mile straight down!

Unlike the relatively easy placer mining operations that had been utilized successfully in California for years, Nevada mining efforts required the digging of deep shafts and offshooting tunnels, many of them blasted with agonizing slowness through solid rock. Further complicating the recovery procedure was the fact that the surrounding earth had a tendency to shift and the body of ore itself was amazingly soft. Cave-ins were commonplace.

By 1860, when they should have been booming, most mining operations on the Comstock had ground suddenly to a halt. At a time when investors were expecting peak returns, the mountain was yielding little. The silver was there, alright; no doubt about it. There simply was no safe way to get to it. In frustration, a coalition of mine owners sent an urgent message to Phillip Deidesheimer.

The first few weeks in Nevada were frustrating for the engineer. Time and time again, he would descend into the Ophir Mine (a claim originally staked out by Henry Comstock himself) only to return to the surface without a solution. Timbers could be used, of course, but the shifting earth would shove them aside almost as quickly as they could be put in place. Wooden beams, 12 inches square, snapped like kindling wood in the hands of a giant. Deidesheimer was stymied.

It was then that a honeybee came to the rescue.

He had been staring dejectedly out across the barren landscape when he chanced to notice a bee darting among the blooming sagebrush. Fascinated, he followed the bee and came upon a hive. There before him was the answer. Deidesheimer would build a honeycomb, a honeycomb of timber. He was certain the concept could work.

And it did.

Within a week, the engineer had fashioned cubes made entirely of timbers and had them lowered one at a time into the depths of the Ophir. Once they were dropped to the desired level, the cubes were dragged along by mules and slid into place. The resulting puzzle-like structure held. Deidesheimer's honeycomb, quickly dubbed a "square set," would revolutionize underground mining methods forever.

Eventually the German became the Superintendent of the Ophir and through considerable inside information was able to amass a sizeable fortune in the stock market. But his success was short lived. Soon, the market plummeted. Deidesheimer was wiped out. He abandoned his great achievement and moved west to San Francisco.

Next, he experimented with a plan to bring water from Lake Tahoe to San Francisco but the scheme fell by the wayside for lack of financing. By the turn of the century he had begun selling real estate. Then came the 1906 earthquake.

Phillip Deidesheimer died at age 84 in dire financial straits.

Ironically, he could have been fabulously wealthy. In his twilight years he was asked why he had failed to patent the "honeycomb" concept of underground mining. His reply was simple, much like the man himself, and showed his dedication:

"If all goes well and those square sets protect the lives of the miners, what more could a man ask for?"

Little did he realize that his amazing feat of engineering, accomplished with the help of a lowly honeybee, had revolutionized underground mining forever, assuring a bright future for the Silver State for years to come...

A TALE OF TWO HATS
-12-

Have you noticed how 'clinic' conscious we are today? I mean, we seem to have a clinic for everything.

Are you drinking too much? Are drugs ruining your life? Do you want to quit smoking? Is you wife/son/daughter/husband having problems adjusting to sex/life/death/themselves?

"Somebody cares," coo the ads, "Just check into our friendly neighborhood clinic and our courteous staff will promptly put you back on the road to the good life!"

Those commercials really bug me. They tout an easy solution to complicated and often delicate emotional or dependency problems. And what they neglect to tell you in all the slick advertising is that your little sojourn to that friendly neighborhood clinic could cost you tens of thousands of dollars.

There are plenty of legitimate reasons, of course, for seeking competent, professional counseling. But there is a fine dividing line between what we are able to do for ourselves and what we need others to do for us. After all, human beings are admittedly pretty weak characters, if you believe all the propaganda. Additionally, these institutions offer the services of some of the best people around. Still, I'm seeing something on the far horizon I call the "clinic syndrome" and it worries me a bit.

A lot of influential people are behind this trend, perhaps without even knowing it. For example, when Betty Ford came out of the closet and proclaimed to the masses that she had a drinking problem, the entire world sat up to take notice. Soon major stars such as Elizabeth Taylor were extolling the virtues of being alcohol-free. Whenever you picked up a newspaper, there was yet another story about another celebrity who had taken "the cure." It's become so commonplace that when Mrs. Dukakis checked in after the recent presidential campaign, hardly an eyebrow was raised.

But in the early days of the Silver State, clinics had yet to be invented. Even your friendly country sawbones (you remember him, the fellah who used to stop by the house, trusty bag in hand. You paid him in chickens), often told you to "take your problems by the horns and ride it out."

And, surprisingly enough, sometimes that ancient philosophy actually worked. Take the case of Okie McGillicuty.

Okie was a rounder of epic proportions. He lived in Winnemucca back in the '30's and each night he and a few of his friends would do their damndest to drink the town dry. Most of the time they succeeded. But each night Okie would pass out and that's when the trouble began.

Ever tried to lug a 285 pound drunk up a flight of stairs? Well, such was the unwelcome task of Okie's two friends. Each night they had to drag the limp carcass of Okie McGillicuty up the back stairs of the Winnemucca Hotel and put him to bed.

It was only a matter of time before they got mighty tired of their nightly weight lifting. Talking to Okie didn't seem to work. What to do? His friends decided to scare the hell out of Okie McGillicuty, and the "cure" they dreamed up was pure genius, Nevada-style.

They began innocently enough, by commenting casually that it seemed like Okie "could use himself a new hat". Sure enough, after a week or so of this gentle harassment, Okie decided to trade in his battered Stetson for a new 4X beaver and, friends in tow, he headed off to the general store. The sale complete and with the new hat perched proudly on his curly head, Okie suggested a friendly libation. His friends politely, but firmly, declined.

Now here the plot thickens.

As soon as Okie had headed off to the safety of the nearest saloon, his friends returned to the mercantile and purchased two more hats —both exactly like the one that had been sold to McGillicuty with one small exception. One hat was two sizes smaller and the other two sizes larger. Aha, you're catching on, aren't you?

So the trap was set.

Hiding the other new hats safely away, the friends joined their jovial companion for their usual night on the town. From hotel to saloon, from saloon to hotel, they hit every watering hole in Winnemucca and sure enough shortly after midnight, Okie

McGillicuty went crashing to the floor and was carried unceremoniously up to bed.

But as soon as he was tucked away, his friends (You guessed it!) switched hats, removing his brand new Stetson and replacing it with another that, this time, was two sizes too small.

At daybreak the conspirators were waiting patiently when Okie came down the stairs. There perched precariously atop his head was a Stetson that barely came down to his forehead. A good laugh was had by all as they reminisced about the night before with Okie believing for all the world that perhaps his head was swelling "just a bit."

The next night was a repeat. But this time when Okie was safely under the covers, the hats were switched again, and this time the 'new' hat was the one that was two sizes too big. When Okie descended the stairs the following morning, his hat was completely down over his ears.

History doesn't record how many times this little scenario was repeated. But Winnemucca old timers agree that Okie McGillicuty soon gave up drinking for good. (Author's note: by now perhaps you've surmised that that was not his real name)

You see, he had become thoroughly convinced that his drinking had given him an incurable case of something known as "alcoholaremia", a condition, then, as now, non-existent. His friends had assured him the dreaded "disease" caused "an abrupt swelling and shrinkage of the skull."

The ruse worked. Okie McGillicuty eventually became a tee-totaler and he went on to become quite an upstanding citizen of the northern part of our state.

So the next time you or a friend or relative seems to have a problem that needs a little cure, why not take a page from Nevada history?

Before you send your friend to a clinic, try scaring the hell out of him instead...

"The citizens inhabiting the valleys within the Great Basin of the American Continent beg leave respectively to present for the consideration of the President of the United States and both houses of Congress their petition praying for the organization of a new Territory of the United States. We do not propose to come with any flourish of trumpets but to simply submit a few plain statements as inducements to those who have the power to remedy the difficulties and embarrassments under which we now labor and suffer.

"A large portion of the inhabitants making this appeal to the powers that be in Washington have been in the region for the past 6 or 7 years without any Territorial, State or Federal protection from Indian depredations and marauding outlaws, runaway criminals and convicts as well as evildoers.

—A letter drafted by early Nevada settlers—
Genoa, Utah Territory, 1857

TRIBUTE TO A MINER...
-13-

"Seize him by the coattails, roll him in the mud. Let into him with pick handles that he may kick the bucket. They have kicked the bully miner, they have dunked him in a ditch.

"He has outpacked the Dutch peddler and he has traveled more than a candidate for Congress. He is older than Washoe butter; he is younger than the beef. He has drunk more than there are shares in the Comstock.

"He fights like a tiger and sings like a canary. It is he who sees the first peep of dawn through the bottom of a tumbler. It is he who carries the pan, the pick and the shovel.

"Thou will, one day, cease to carry the sacks of specimens on your broad shoulders. But as long as thou art remembered, thou shalt not be forgotten. Bully, the honest miner!"

Those words were written 125 years ago at a time when the miner was king, literally. You see, Nevada is a child of the mining industry, a fact sadly forgotten in the most recent go-around of the State Legislature. The miner has been Nevada's backbone since the 1850's.

You better treat him nice, too, because he is fast becoming so again.

The first miners to come to Nevada were not really miners at all. Known as "49'ers," after the year in which the first gold was discovered near Sutter's Mill in northern California, they actually spent very little of their time underground. Rather, they moved from place to place, searching for that elusive something, that tiny glint of color, that sparkle of crumbling quartz. When they found it, they panned what little they could and moved on.

Comstock journalist Alf Doten described the 49'er this way: "He was a short, square built old youngster, with grizzled hair and a beard that had seen no other trimming than his trusty old knife could do. His dilapidated brown felt hat had a peculiar jaunty old mash over the larboard side of his head. One trouser leg was in his boot and the other usually wasn't. No overcoat obscured the old grey flannel shirt he wore.

"His trusty old doubled barreled shotgun was slung under his left arm and held in place with a bit of baling rope. An old briar pipe was in his mouth.

"He led a quiet-looking sorrel horse, well-packed with canvas tent, cooking utensils, pick, shovel and such. He cast a sort of practical glance at the street and buildings as he went by, as he had in hundreds of other towns, many of which have died long ago. He didn't worry much about a night's lodging. He was far more content on the ground.

But he wouldn't remain that way long.

In Nevada, the prospector found wealth far more elusive than in California. The gold wasn't "just lying around," glittering up from a forgotten creekbed or jutting out from under a rainswept overhang. Nevada's gold and silver was deep underground. Suddenly the prospector had become a miner, and, by necessity, suddenly more resourceful.

Over the next 50 years, he would learn how to build tunnels miles deep into the dark belly of the earth by fashioning a series of honeycomb-like structures that would be copied by miners the world over. He would learn to bring precious water not just down from the mountains as had been done for centuries, but up to the mines from the valley floor, using nothing more than the force of gravity to accomplish a task that most said "couldn't be done!"

The work was back-breaking, even tortureous, the working conditions even worse. Enduring temperatures that sometimes rose to more than 130 degrees at the 1000 feet level, he would labor through an eight hour shift, taking only short breaks to eat, drink and chew ice to keep his body from boiling itself alive.

He chose one of three shifts; the morning, beginning at 7 a.m., the afternoon, which began at 3, or the graveyard shift which ran from 11 p.m. until 7 in the morning.

But despite the stories about the Comstock's fabulous riches, food and lodging was so expensive that many a miner had difficulty making ends meet. Although he was among the highest paid hard rock workers in the world (with wages of up to $5.00 a day) 4/5's of his weekly salary went for lodging, leaving very little left for a meal, which averaged 50 cents.

Yet, the miner was generous, almost to a fault. During the half century that he worked deep underground, he gave away millions, —some went to visiting performers, some went to his friendly bartender, but much of his take went to care for his own.

When a brother was killed (and roughly 10,000 men were maimed or killed in the mines of Virginia City), it was not at all unusual for those in the mines to put up a purse of as much as $1500.00 for the widow and the surviving children. That was the rough equivalent of 4 year's pay, a more-than-generous gesture to say the least.

A small donation was usually made immediately, a few hundred dollars to "tide you over." Then, on the first of the next month, the traditional payday, each worker would turn back to his paymaster a dollar or two. In this fashion, a sizeable amount could be raised in no time.

By the turn of the century, however, most of Nevada's miners had gone off to greener pastures, as had the 49'ers before them. From the Comstock, it was on to Montana, Colorado, Alaska and Arizona, to other booms and other busts, to other bonanzas and other dreams. Some would strike it big, this time in central and southern Nevada. Places like Tonopah and Goldfield sprung up. But those towns too, despite their awesome riches, soon faded away as well.

Bonanza became borrasca. Again, it was time for the miner to move on.

For more than half a century, most of the miners have been gone from the Silver State. Oh, a few have remained, of course, still searching the desert wastelands and the prehistoric creekbeds. But for the most part, the underground miner has abandoned the place where it had all began.

Today, however, the times they are a'changin'. With new and improved methods of extraction now available, mining has become profitable once again. In addition, it is estimated that there is still so much wealth remaining here in Nevada that the original Comstock could pale by comparison.

So remember the early miner. He built Nevada more than 125 years ago, built it from sagebrush and desolation into a state known for luck and quick riches throughout the world.

Very soon, he may come to our rescue again.

At a time when our tourism industry is up against some pretty tough competition, we would do well to welcome him with open arms...

THERE'S A PIECE OF THE ROCK RIGHT HERE IN NEVADA!
-14-

Remember those television commercials?

They're a thinly disguised attempt to sell you insurance. There it is, the Rock of Gibraltor, moving slowly, majestically, across America, through golden fields of wheat and along super highways, across raging rivers and even smack dab down the center of the Wall Street financial district. It makes good commercial television, I suppose, but it ain't gonna convince me to buy insurance.

But did you know there's a piece of the rock right here in Nevada? Not a piece of the Rock of Gibraltor, mind you, but not just any old rock either. It's a piece of the famed Plymouth Rock. You know, the one the Pilgrims landed on when they decided that they had had enough of the Atlantic Ocean.

And therein lies the tale...

The story begins back in 1862. One Major E.A. Sherman, formerly of Bridgewater, Massachusetts, had just opened the first newspaper in the booming mining camp of Aurora. He called it the Esmeralda Star and, as frontier newspapers go, it was quite a hit. He covered the latest silver and gold strikes, the most recent shootouts and even a hanging or two.

The Civil War was raging at the time and in the mining camps of early Nevada, most of the population was divided in their sympathies. But few bothered to give the War more than a passing interest. After all, they were in the midst of a gold and silver boom —the grand-daddy of them all, some said —and most Nevadans were quite content to let the 'Easterners' take care of the situation themselves. They were concerned, yes. But few men were about to pull up such fabulous stakes and head east simply for a chance to take a bullet in the chest.

But Major Sherman was the exception. He was a staunch

defender of the Union cause and decided that if the miners could not support the conflict in person, the least they could do would be to support it with some financing.

At the time, the most popular charity in the country was something called the Sanitary Commission, actually the forerunner of the modern-day Red Cross. Sherman suggested that the good citizens of Aurora pony up some money for the commission and he said so in no uncertain terms. Daily, in his headlines, he ranted and raved, he puffed and he panted. He tried everything short of outright blackmail to raise the money.

But when funds were slow in coming, the wily Sherman devised an ingenious scheme. Being a native of Massachusetts, he was on friendly terms with descendents of some of the original Pilgrims who had landed that fateful day in Plymouth. More important, he knew that Easterners, though caught up in the violent war effort, were still fascinated by the stories emanating from Nevada, stories that told of the fabulous wealth of the Comstock.

So he managed to rustle up a huge 50-pound chunk of quartz that was laced liberally with gold and silver. With ore in hand, he boarded the eastbound train for Massachusetts.

There, the ingenious Sherman traded his hunk of Nevada ore for a piece of the original Plymouth Rock. Amazingly enough, in the process he even managed to make the Easterners think they got the better end of the bargain. Sherman promptly headed back to Nevada with his coveted prize.

In Aurora, he held a series of auctions and the townspeople purchased the rock not once, but several times. The miners might not have chosen to fight, but few could say that they were not patriotic Americans.

The auctions proved to be a tremendous success. In an act which spoke proudly of their great community spirit, the men donated the rock back to the city to be used in the construction of a new courthouse. With much pomp and circumstance, it was carefully cemented in place. The future of Aurora, many thought, was assured.

But as was so often the case in early Nevada, the brightness of the future proved fleeting at best. For Aurora, it would be no more than two short years before the ore supply was depleted. The miners moved on, leaving the town to the harshness of the elements. Wooden buildings soon decayed and what few stone buildings had been erected were slowly dismantled, stone by stone, for use elsewhere.

And that piece of the rock? Well, believe it or not, it's still out there somewhere. During the construction of the original courthouse, the workers had neglected to label it, and like so many other stones, it was simply carted off to a new place and another purpose.

So if you're passing through northern Nevada (experts are convinced it is still somewhere within 50 miles of early Aurora) and you happen to spy one of those picturesque old stone fences or perhaps a dilapidated barn with a beautiful stone foundation, I'd suggest you take a closer look.

You might have just come upon a piece of the rock. And this time, it could be the REAL one!

"The Indians are broken up into many bands. The Paiutes are much the largest in number, being about 40,000. They are not hostile to Americans and have never favored the Mormons. They are friendly towards the new territory and indeed anxious for it. They desire to cultivate the arts of peace and become tillers of the soil.

"They are the best servants in America and have shown themselves to be excellent cooks, farmers, herdsmen and mechanics. All the other tribes are warlike, insincere, treacherous and blood thirsty. Should the Territory be organized, the Paiutes would promptly unite with the whites and identify themselves with the peaceful progress of the country.

—Sacramento State Journal—
1857

THE PRESS CORP
OF RAWHIDE...
-15-

A lot has happened in this state over the past century and a quarter.

Born on the slopes of Mount Davidson, Nevada grew to become a miner's paradise, a place that has captured the imagination of the entire world. When one boomtown went bust, another sprung up to take its place.

More recently, in the past 30 years or so, mining has been eclipsed, of course, by tourism, particularly gaming, as the state's number one industry. But some things still remain the same. Both mining and gambling needed promotion in their infancy. Today they still do.

Ever read the tabloids that many of the casinos and restaurants give out? They are usually slick publications like Fun and Gaming, Showtime, Entertainment, and in them you'll read tales of fabulous jackpots awarded to lucky casino patrons, some of whom have become, quite literally, instant millionaires. You'll find stories about the biggest names in show business, about the brightest stars of stage and screen. That's what these publications are all about, they are a potpourri of the "good life" that could be there for all of us. If, that is, we're lucky.

These exciting and tantalizing little ditties, of course, have been cranked out by casino public relations people. For the most part good writers, their job is to chronicle the excitement and the pizzazz of the casino industry and to do it in such a way that stirs the blood, that makes folks want to get in on the "action."

Well, nothing has changed in 80 years. The boomtown of Rawhide is a case in point.

While there were no "P.R." publications per se in the fledgling city back in 1907 and 1908, there were pr people galore. "Correspondents" from across the nation flooded the city. Armed with the certain knowledge that people everywhere were eager to hear about the latest strike and the fabulous wealth that seemed to abound everywhere in the west, they actually cranked out more stories than casinos do today.

This article appeared in a San Francisco paper on February 19, 1908: "W.H. Scott of the Goldfield Brokerage House of Scott and Amann, who returned from Rawhide this morning, expresses the opinion that within a year that camp will be the largest gold producer in the state. 'When a man is broke in Rawhide,' says Mr. Scott, 'he can always eat. All he has to do is go to some lease and pan out breakfast money. There is rich ore on every dump, and every man is made welcome!'"

The story, of course, was a plant, designed specifically to trigger interest among mining speculators. Still, the correspondents of Rawhide continued to pound out their stories of richness. One H. W. Knickerbocker filed this report for a Reno paper.

"Gold! Gold! Gold! The wise men of old sought alchemy whereby they could transmute the base metals into gold. It was a fruitless quest then; it is a needless quest now. Rawhide has been discovered!"

I love this next part. This writer obviously missed his calling. He could have made a helluva poet. "No flowers bloom upon her rock-ribbed bosom. No dimpling streams kiss her soil into verdure, to flash in laminated silver 'neath the sunbeams touch. No flowers nor food, no beauty or utility on the surface; but from her desert-covered heart Rawhide is pouring a stream of yellow gold out upon the world which is translatable, not simply into food and houses and comfort, but also into pictures and poetry and music and all those things that minister in an objective way to the development of a full-orbed manhood."

How's that for making a silk purse out of a sow's ear? Today this guy would be working on Lifestyles of the Rich and Famous.

J. S. Jordan forwarded the following dispatch to not one, but a string of west coast newspapers.

"Right through what is now the main street of Rawhide, in the days of '49, the makers of California passed on their way to the new Eldorado. They had many hardships through which to pass before reaching the gold which was their lure, and thousands went through the hills of Rawhide never reaching their goal. They were massacred by Indians, or fell victim to the thirst and heat of the

4 6

desert and for many years the way across the plains was marked by the whitening bones of the pathfinders. Here in Rawhide, all the while, lay the treasures of Captain Kidd, the ransoms of crowns!"

Public relations man Harry Hedrick was no less enthusiastic: "To stand on 20 different claims each day as I have done; to take the virgin rock from the ledge, to reduce it to a pulp and then to watch a string of saint-reducing dross encircle the pan; to peer over the shoulder of the assayer while he takes the precious button from the crucible —these are the convincing things about this newest and greatest of gold camps."

Then he really got rolling.

"It is not a novelty to have assays run into the thousands. In fact, it is commonplace. To report strikes of a few hundred dollars to the ton seems, in Rawhide, like an anticlimax."

Yep, just as the tourism industry today peppers the press with stories of gigantic jackpots, the mining interests of old were no slouches themselves when it came to public relations.

And while some of you might say, "Aw, it's all hype!," that's only partially true.

Those jackpots and bonanzas are still out there.

Somewhere.

You need only a little bit of luck to find them...

THE CAPTURE OF
ELINOR GLYN
-16-

It was late in the year, almost 1910 in Rawhide.

There were two things about the city that were making headlines. One was the fact that Rawhide was gaining the reputation as one of the richest mining towns in the entire west, richer still than Tonopah, greater even than Goldfield.

The other was Elinor Glyn.

The mining news was important, certainly, but it paled next to the furor over the talented and attractive author of the best selling novel *Three Weeks*. Glyn was the toast of two continents, the most famous writer in the world.

She was also vacationing in San Francisco. If somehow, she could be persuaded to make a little sidetrip to Rawhide... Gosh, the famous Elinor Glyn. In Rawhide. Why, it would make every newspaper in the country...

Ray Baker was sent to do the job. Baker, a handsome, flamboyant Nevada bon vivant, was told, "Please suggest to [Mrs. Glyn] the advisability of visiting Rawhide. The lady can get much local color for a new book. If you bag the game you will be a hero!"

Baker knew it and he wasted little time. Within a few days, he had introduced himself to the authoress. Thirty-eight hours later, after a hectic ride by train and automobile, he escorted her grandly into a wildly cheering Rawhide.

But the real show was only about to begin.

That evening, it was suggested that Glyn be shown a real Nevada saloon, perhaps watch a game a stud poker, a REAL game, as played out on the desert. Author George Rice picks up the story from there.

"They entered a room. Six players were seated around a table. The men were coatless and grimy. Their unshaven mugs, rough as nutmeg graters, were twisted into strange grimaces. All of them appeared the worse for liquor. Before each man was piled a mound of ivory chips of various hues, and alongside rested a six shooter. From the rear trouser's pocket of every player another gun protruded. Each man wore a belt filled with cartridges.

"A man with bloodshot eyes shuffled and rippled the cards. Then he dealt a hand to each.

"'Bet $10,000.' declared the first player.

"'Call that and go you $15,000 better!' shouted the second as he pushed a stack of yellows toward the center'.

"'Raise you!', cried two others, almost in unison.

A gigantic mound of chips began to grow in the middle of the table. "Before the jackpot was played out, $300,000 in chips had found its way to the center of the table and 4 men were standing up in their seats in a frenzy of bravado with the muzzles of their guns viciously pointed at one another. There was enough of the lurking devil in the eyes of the belligerents to give the onlookers a nervous shiver. When the gun play started, Mrs. Glyn and Baker took to the tall and uncut.

The "gun play" erupted with sudden intensity, and as they fled, Ray Baker and the frightened author could hear the entire saloon reverberate with the deafening blasts from every sixgun. Moments later, two stretchers, each solemnly bearing a "corpse" were carried up the street to the undertakers. A terrified Mrs. Glyn stood trembling in horror.

But what she did not know was that she had just witnessed one of the finest charades ever perpetrated in the annals of the old west. The high stakes card game, the "gun play" and the resulting "deaths" -all had been intricately staged, a violent one-act play designed solely to peak the author's excitement and to guarantee "miles of newsprint."

The ruse worked. Wrote Rice, "The camp got yards of publicity that was calculated to convince the public that "Rawhide" was no flash in the pan, which was exactly what was wanted.

Though they were hardly necessary, in the weeks following the "gun fight", even more "events" were staged for the benefit of the now-intrigued Mrs. Glyn.   One evening the town was suddenly awakened by the sound of the dreaded fire bell. A pile of waste lumber and some deserted shacks had erupted into golden flames and the entire town, including the terrified Mrs. Glyn, turned out. The fierce yells of the firemen drowned in the wild stampede of men, horses and equipment.

All of a sudden shouts came from inside one of the blazing shacks. A man in the crowd rushed to the cabin and, without hesitation, dove headlong into the midst of the conflagration. He never came out again.

Mrs. Glyn, and the nation's press, were dazzled. Such heroism in the boomtown of Rawhide!

But what she and the rest of the nation never realized was that 3 feet behind the front door of that burning cabin was a hidden passage leading to an underground tunnel, a tunnel which emptied itself safely into the hills a hundred yards away.

The "capture" of the illustrious Elinor Glyn was a smashing success. Soon she departed, leaving a trail of news accounts of her "great experiences" in rough and tumble Rawhide to follow her across the remainder of the nation.

Mining, not manipulation, soon returned to the headlines in Rawhide. But Elinor Glyn's stay, and the publicity that resulted, went down in the history books as one of Nevada's greatest "P.R." coups.

She was the most famous personage of her day. And she opened in the boomtown of Rawhide.

Just goes to show you the value of bringing in big name entertainment.

Do you suppose that's why Nevada still does it today???

"I had always a desire to go there. My brother was there. In the afternoon when his work was done, he would go about on the hillsides and pick up two or three pailsful of nuggets of gold and silver and by the by, he would become very rich."

—Mark Twain—
Before coming to the Nevada Territory.

"From one extremity of this desert to the other, the road was white with the bones of oxen and horses. The desert was one prodigious graveyard. We could have walked the last 40 miles and set our feet upon a bone at every step.

—Mark Twain—
Upon arrival

THE DISCOVERY OF TONOPAH.
MORE THAN A LEGEND
-17-

Author G.B. Glassock tells the story. He heard it from one Slim Ludwick, the discoverer of the town of Rochester, back in the late 1920's.

"Friend of mine was testifyin' for the defense in a case before Judge Stratton at Buckhorn once," related Slim. "The lawyer for the defense was tryin' to qualify him as an expert witness, an' asked him how long he'd been a prospector. 'Thirty years,' he says. Well, pretty soon the prosecutin' attorney gets to cross-examine him.

"'How many years have you prospected?' he asks.

"''Bout 5 years,' says the witness.

"'Ah ha!' says the prosecutor, lookin' mean an' successful. 'Your Honor, I'd like to have you note that the witness under oath has already said he has been a prospector for 30 years an' now he says he's prospected 5 years.'

"'Wait a minute, wait a minute,' says the witness. 'I said I'd been a prospector for 30 years an' I have. I said I'd prospected 5 years an' I have. Both statements are facts, your Honor. 5 years I prospected and the other 25 I spent lookin' for my burros. You know how it is, your Honor.'

"'The witness qualifies as an expert, ' says the j.p., thereby qualifyin' himself as a judge.

Such tales were commonplace around the campfires of Nevada during the early days of the twentieth century. But this one has more than a little basis in fact. Nevada had entered a 20 year period of deep depression after the mines of Virginia City sputtered and died around 1880. Virtually half of the state's population had left for greener pastures, for places with more exciting names.

But surprisingly enough some stayed, though few can say why. They raised their grubstakes, loaded their burros and trudged off into the searing heat or the freezing cold of the Nevada wilderness.

Something was in their blood, for there can be no other explanation.

They wandered this time into the desolation that was central Nevada, into the Toiyabe, the Monitor, the Hot Creek and the Cactus mountain ranges. There were a few automobiles; they were a rarity. There wasn't a railroad within twenty thousand square miles. It is estimated that each man had six thousand acres all to himself.

Into this sparse and barren landscape came one James Butler, an American born in Logtown, California, a tiny mining camp on the western slopes of the Sierras that today exists only in memory. He found Nye County, and Belmont, the capitol, to his liking. The county encompassed an area roughly double the size of the state of Massachusetts. There was plenty of breathing room. Here he established a small ranch which provided for most of his wants, particularly the urge to wander off into the low-lying hills to search for gold.

Old timers who met Butler called him lazy, but the term was hardly one of disrespect. In fact, "Big" Jim was extremely popular with many in the region who shared his "proper respect for leisure." Still, being lazy did not mean overlooking an opportunity when it arose. Making note of an opening in county government, he applied for the position and was accepted. Jim Butler, rancher and itinerant prospector, suddenly found himself the District Attorney of Nye County.

The job was ideal for Butler. There was little crime in the sparsely populated area and the position did not require membership in the State Bar, a technicality which would have obviously prevented his acceptance. But it did pay the princely sum of $50.00 in scrip which could be cashed on a monthly basis for $35.00. That $35.00 could outfit a prospector handsomely.

It was on one of his frequent trips into the wilderness, on a sojourn to the camp known as Southern Klondike, that Butler struck the big one. His find was the stuff of which legends are made.

Just over the Manhattan Mountains he reached a point which the Indians referred to as Tonopah, a name, some said, which indicated a species of desert growth which usually sprung from a hidden spring. But as Butler prepared to bed down for the night, his burros, as was their wont, strayed off.

Old timer Charlie Higgins claimed that Butler had been

careless. "A handful of barley will keep 'em in easy reach of camp at all times," he explained. He went on to suggest that sharing flapjacks with the four footed creatures worked equally as well.

But Butler's burros strayed nonetheless. By the time he had located them, a blinding duststorm had swept into the region. The prospector and his beasts took shelter beneath an outcropping and settled in to wait out the fury of the sudden storm. As he sat, Jim Butler chipped away idly at the rock. It was May 19th, give or take a week or two, and the year was 1900.

Jim Butler was in no hurry. He never was. When the storm ended, he collected some samples he had broken from the outcropping and continued leisurely on into Southern Klondike. There he found several other men, including Cal and Wilson Brougher and Frank Higgs, working a small claim. According to author Glasscock, the conversation went something like this:

"I've got something," said Butler. "15 miles from home." He threw some of his samples to the men.

After a close inspection, Higgs replied, "Wouldn't give you five cents for a ton of it."

"It's got mineral in it," Butler insisted. "Assay it, Higgs, and I'll give you an interest."

"Nothing doing," replied Higgs. "It's worthless." In disgust, he tossed the samples back to Butler. With a shrug, Jim Butler set out on the return trip to Belmont.

But some changes had been made in his absence. An election had come and gone and now Nye County had a new District Attorney, Tasker Oddie. Again, Butler just shrugged off the situation. After all, Oddie was a friend and the loss of his job would just allow Butler more time for exploration. But the fortunes of Oddie and Butler would be entwined from that day forth.

You see, Jim Butler didn't have the money to have his samples assayed, so he offered them to Oddie. Oddie, unfortunately, was in the same dire straights. Nevertheless, on his next trip to Austin, Oddie took the samples along, and after cutting assayer Walter Gayhart in on the partnership, he learned the real truth. The assay left both men gasping for breath. The ore yielded a return of $75.00 a ton! That initial discovery, stumbled upon by Butler's own burros, would net the "lazy" prospector more than $336,000!

Butler was rich and the town of Tonopah sprung up. Tasker Oddie would go on to become Governor of the State of Nevada.

Truth, as they say, is stranger than fiction.

Today there are still those men who have the fever. Today, they venture off into the desert with little more than a dream, and a hazy one at that. Today the 4-wheel drive has replaced the lowly burro, but the dream remains. Old timers say the dream of riches lurks within us all.

Perhaps even you...

THE $30,000.00 BEER KEG
-18-

Saunter along the Las Vegas strip and you'll see how hard the PR guys and gals work to get your attention. Short of committing a felony, they'll do just about anything to get you in those casino doors and for good reason. You're the one who pays the bills. Their accomplishments are legendary. A Las Vegas hotel once sunk a craps table in their outdoor swimming pool, dressed the dealers in bathing trunks and made national headlines with their "floating craps game". The old Cal-Neva Lodge at the north shore of Lake Tahoe, once the stronghold of entertainer Frank Sinatra, got people to sit up and take notice when they physically painted the California/Nevada state line right through the middle of the joint —even underwater, straight across the bottom of the swimming pool. The folks at John Ascuaga's Nugget in Sparks once took their famous performing elephants for a little swim in Reno's Virginia Lake. The idea drew more publicity than planned. The elephants decided they liked their new "swimming hole" and wouldn't come out again. It was all great fun.

But such is the stuff of which legends are made. I have a theory that a good public relations person never sleeps. Subconsciously, like the Bloom County character with his anxiety closet, the mind of a good "P.R." person is always dreaming up something —like it or not.

But modern public relations types have nothing on one Leo Hetchinger, an itinerant Virginia City miner back during the heyday of the Comstock. Leo decided that he could make more money gambling than mining, and he was right. But what he really needed was some kind of a gimmick...

At the time, the life of an underground miner was anything but desirable. While there were plenty of romantic stories about how riches could be "had for the taking," in actuality, nothing was

5 5

further from the truth. The shifts were grueling, shafts were unbelievably cramped and, at some depths, temperatures soared to more than 120 degrees. The work was both back-breaking and dangerous. While the pay was good, the cost of living in the booming mining town (a single egg would bring a dollar!) left little in a miner's poke.

It was boredom that generally took the biggest toll. Female companionship was usually limited to ladies of uncertain virtue and the only true recreation, until an opera house was built, was drinking to excess in one of the more than 100 local saloons. To alleviate the problem, the men would stage contests —boxing matches, cockfights, bull and bear fights, arm wrestling, anything to combat the daily routine of work, drink, sleep and work again. That gave Leo Hetchinger an idea...

The wiry German had but two passions in life: drinking beer and making a friendly wager. One day he simply decided to combine the two. He challenged any and all comers: He would hoist an oaken beer keg high on his shoulder and carry it right up to the top of Mount Davidson. And back down again.

Keep in mind this way no mean feat. Even today, in this age of physical fitness mania, the attempt seems monumental. The distance was more than 2 miles, over terrain that was, in many cases, almost vertical. The keg itself weighed more than 100 pounds.

But the most important factor was the altitude. It approached 7,000 feet. To top it off, Hetchinger himself was a scrawny little fellow, weighing less than 140 pounds soaking wet. All these factors combined to create quite an attractive betting situation. The wagers began to roll in.

But Hetchinger was not content to leave anything to chance. He took out an ad in the Territorial Enterprise claiming that he would "take on all comers" and he would accept all individual bets of "up to $3500.00," a fabulous sum even for Virginia City. To emphasize his point, he donned an ape-man suit, a loincloth affair that showed off his spindly frame "to perfection" and paraded through the saloons accepting the bets in person.

The day of the event a huge banner was hung across the street and the saloons were filled to overflowing. With all the bravado of a young Mohammed Ali, Hetchinger jogged up and down the streets in his loincloth, pausing in front of each saloon to drink a beer and accept a bet or two. When the gun sounded, he hefted the beer keg and took off at a trot straight up the mountain.

He returned to the finish line in just over two hours. His progress had been monitored all along the way, and it was reported that he was delayed hardly at all by the rough terrain and the treacherous outcroppings of jagged rock. Although he was sweating profusely, he hardly seemed winded at all.

Reluctantly, the crowd of miners pushed forward to pay off their bets and Hetchinger retired to the nearest saloon to toast his winnings with the very beer he had just carried to the mountaintop on his back. It was the stuff public relations men only dream about. "Man with Beer Keg Climbs Silver Mountain!" screamed the headlines.

Leo Hetchinger made himself $30,000.00 that day in Virginia City, and many thought that their eyes had deceived them. After all, how could such a little man carry a 100-pound beer keg up that mountain and back again? It just wasn't possible.

But what they didn't know was that Leo Hetchinger had never for a moment doubted he could do it. In fact, he was absolutely certain that he could. You see, under the cover of darkness, just one month before, the wily little German had already done it. And not once, mind you, but twice!

Practice definitely makes perfect!

"There are no inhabitants in the region at all, save those who are charged with the mail service. The only things not human seen living are snakes, lizards and crickets, upon which the local Indians are forced to feed for a portion of the year."

—J. P. Waters, U.S. Deputy Marshall—
Upon seeing the Humboldt region for the first time.

A 'PILFERING' REPORTER
ON THE COMSTOCK
-19-

"At the solicitation of about 1500 of our subscribers, we will refrain from ever again entering into a controversy with that beef-eating, blear-eared, hollow-headed, slab-sided ignoramus, that pilfering reporter, Mark Twain." — The Virginia City Evening Bulletin.

Ignoramus? Mark Twain? Were they describing THE Mark Twain? The man soon to become America's favorite author? The man who penned Tom Sawyer, Huckleberry Finn and the Celebrated Jumping Frog of Calavaras County? Naaah, they couldn't be.

But they were.

As every school-aged youngster knows, Mark Twain (or Sam Clemens if you prefer) became the country's most popular writer. To hear Twain himself tell it, he was the best thing to happen to the profession since the invention of the quill pen. This was the man who came west to seek his fortune and escape the Civil War, took a pen name reminiscent of his riverboating days, and went on to fame and fortune as the author of classic, home-grown American literature.

In actuality, however, Twain got his start under rather dubious circumstances. Although later he was fond of lecturing with pride about his boisterous beginnings in Virginia City, he was far from famous at the time. In fact, during his time of the Comstock, by many he was not even particularly well-liked.

Back in the early 1860's Sam Clemens had been mustered out of the Union army. His military career had been undistinguished and he was determined to see what the country was like beyond the confines of his hometown, Hannibal, Missouri. As it happened, his brother Orion had just been appointed Secretary of the Nevada

Territory and Twain decided to go along for the ride.

Arriving in Carson City, he soon set out to seek his fortune, not as a writer, but as a lumber speculator. He formed a partnership with another man and the two attempted to buy up some lush timber property at Lake Tahoe. When the deal fell through, Twain was left penniless. Frustrated, he turned to prospecting, but after many months and numerous personal grubstakes from brother Orion, he failed at that as well. Writing, only a hidden passion up to this point, was the only thing keeping him from the poorhouse.

He began by bombarding western newspapers, particularly the Territorial Enterprise, with 'letters' or short stories from the diggings. Although he signed them simply as "Josh", Enterprise editor Joe Goodman was intrigued. He wired the mystery writer and offered him a job. Less than a month later, Sam Clemens was finally gainfully employed. Soon he was writing regular columns for the Enterprise under an entirely new name, Mark Twain.

Hardly anything that happened in raucous Virginia City managed to escape his considerable wit and wisdom. He was a champion of popular causes, but restless. When Goodman was called away on business, he made Twain the acting editor. It was a decision Joe Goodman who soon live to regret.

As the saying goes, "When the cat's away, the mice will play!", and Twain was no exception. He wrote a lurid account of what he called the "Empire City Massacre", in which he described in great detail how a popular frontier family had been bludgeoned to death by a gone-mad father. It was absolute fiction, but it was taken as gospel by many in the area and the story even found it way into the San Francisco papers. When the truth eventually surfaced, rival newspapers began criticizing the Enterprise for its choice of reporters.

On the 300th birthday of William Shakespeare, he wrote a sonnet and attributed it to the Bard himself. When it finally came to light that the poetry was his, he bragged openly about the deception, claiming "in many respects, it was more important and striking and readable than the real Shakespeare."

As if to add insult to injury, he then decided to pick on the Sanitary Commission of Carson City, a women's auxiliary of the organization that would soon become the American Red Cross. He mimicked the ladies in scathing fashion, describing the dress of one socialite as "set off by bagnettes, boynettes and clarinets", and "well suited to the serene dignity of her bearing."

Unfortunately for the practical joker, the lady turned out to be the wife of one Bill Stewart, a prominent lawyer who would later go on to become a United States Senator. Though Twain and Stewart were friends, the latter had his wife's reputation at stake. He was determined to have revenge: Stewart and several of his friends, posing as robbers, stopped a stagecoach in which Twain was riding and made him dismount. They roughed him up considerably, then threw him off the road and down into a canyon. For good measure, they demolished his suitcase and threw that into the gully as well.

But Twain was undaunted. The following week he wrote still another story, this time about the stage coach robbery at which he himself "had been present." In glowing prose, he claimed that he had been a witness to "the boldest stage holdup to take place in the entire country." He delicately neglected to mention that he himself had been the object of the "robbery."

His practical jokes, though enjoyed immensely by the miners, did not sit well with high society. Eventually Twain sought greener pastures and he left the Comstock for good. His departure was duly noted in the Gold Hill Evening News: "Among the few mortals that departed yesterday we notice the name of Mark Twain. And no wonder. Twain's beard is full of dirt and his face is black before the people of Washoe. He has indulged in the game infernal. He has vamoosed, cut, asquatulated [whatever that means!] and now will tarry among the pine forests of the Sierra or in San Francisco, the city of earthquakes.

"Good riddance!" spat the News, "The office of the Territorial Enterprise will become purified."

Luckily for the young writer from Hannibal, Missouri, he went on to write Tom Sawyer...

PIOCHE
MURDER AND MAYHEM ON
THE EARLY FRONTIER
-20-

They warned him. "No bartender has ever lasted a year in Pioche. You take a job down there and you'll wind up deader than last year's Christmas turkey!"

But Faddiman wouldn't listen. He needed the work and Pioche was booming. Besides, who was to say that he might not come upon a strike that would make him a millionaire? Bartender Faddiman boarded the stage for Pioche. Two weeks later he was dead.

Tombstone. Dodge City. Abilene. They were the rough and tumble towns long celebrated in motion pictures, on television, in story and song. But while not as well known perhaps, the town of Pioche in its heydey was every bit as raucous...and just as deadly.

The town was named for a French trader, F.L. Pioche, who had wandered through the territory prior to the year 1860. Although he didn't know it at the time, the region would yield millions. It would also become a hotbed of violence and murder.

But bartender Faddiman wasn't worried when he stepped off the afternoon stage. After all, he had worked boomtowns before. He knew that the miners were a wild bunch and violence often came with the job. If the barren land and the lack of feminine companionship didn't get you, the boredom would. Faddiman knew that. And he knew that the fellas just needed to blow off a little steam. If a man was careful, everything would be alright.

It was just a little past noon when a man staggered into Faddiman's saloon. Faddiman knew him. He also knew that the man had been down on his luck for quite some time. The effects were obvious; his hands were shaking, his shirt was ragged and perspiration stood out on his cheeks. When the man ordered a drink, Faddiman served him.

It would be the last decision he would ever have to make. The man stepped back from the bar, pulled a pistol from his belt and shot Faddiman point blank in the chest.

From the saloon, the killer ran next door to a butcher shop owned by a woman known only to the town as Nigger Liza. She refused to hide him and, brandishing a butcher knife, ordered him from her shop. He seized the blade and savagely slit her throat.

By this time word of the Faddiman killing had reached the deputy sheriff. Learning that the miner had fled into the butcher shop, the deputy positioned himself across the street. As the killer stepped out on to the boardwalk, the lawman unloaded his pistol, killing the miner instantly. Such was justice in early Pioche.

The town had grown up peacefully enough. In fact one of the earliest strikes had come about because friendly Indians in the area had been anxious to help their new white neighbors. Prospector Bill Hambin had been led to a rich outcropping of ore by a local Indian who had no interest in the flashy metal. Hambin, who took more pleasure in finding a claim than it working it, sold out within weeks to a French investor. Ironically, that ledge would eventually be worth more than $40 million.

As bartender Faddiman well knew, violence in the early boomtowns "came with the territory." Just as the strikes lured honest men to seek their fortunes, they also attracted men who chose to make their living off the labor of others. It was said that during the first year of its existence, the cemetery of Pioche hosted not a single person who had died of natural causes.

And Boot Hill seemed to bear this out. Unlike most cemeteries at the time, the one in Pioche was actually divided into sections, each with its own name to signify the manner of demise — Murderer's Row, Hangman's Gulch and so on.

One hot August day a local prospector was shot and killed by two men intent on jumping his claim. The prospector, whose name is lost to history, was a popular character with the townsfolk and particularly with the town's deputy sheriff. The men were in custody within hours.

But the arresting officer didn't bother with a trial. He marched the men straight up to Murderer's Row, the section of the graveyard reserved for men of just such persuasion. There he forced the pair to dig two graves. Once the holes were dug, the deputy read a few choice words over the spot, shot the grave diggers in the chest and quietly rolled the bodies into the freshly dug holes. Justice, if not honest, was swift.

A story is told of a young Eastern lawyer who had arrived in town with his new bride to defend a man accused of murder. As they alighted from the stage they were greeted immediately by gunfire. Unwittingly, they had been caught in a crossfire between lawmen and a group of alleged claimjumpers. No one was hurt in the exchange, but the lawyer and his wife promptly reboarded the stage and were never seen again.

If the story is true, it was perhaps the best move the young lawyer ever made, for such violence was a way of life in early Pioche.

The best testament of all was the graveyard itself. In an isolated, unmarked portion of the cemetery were more than 100 graves. Without exception each one held the remains of a killer, a killer who died before civilization came to the Nevada frontier.

"There were numerous sales of mining claims almost daily, at what then was thought to be high prices, and the hundreds who were unprovided with money with which to purchase mining ground swarmed the hills in search of ledges that were still undiscovered and unclaimed. The whole country was supposed to be full of silver lodes as rich as the Comstock, and the man who was so fortunate as to find a large unoccupied vein containing a color similar to that of the Ophir considered his fortune made."

—Virginia City reporter Dan DeQuille—
Describing the aftermath of the initial silver strike.

FROM RAGS TO RICHES
AND BACK AGAIN
-21-

Allison Orrum was a comely lass. She had emigrated from Scotland as a youngster and soon found herself on the Comstock, the wife of a Mormon named Steve Hunter. Little did she know she would soon become one of the richest women in America.

Gold Hill;, or Gold Canyon as it was then known, was hardly living up to its name. When Allison Orrum arrived, the most anyone had taken from the ground was a meager $5.00 a day. While that was extremely good pay back in the late 1850's, to prospectors dreaming of the big bonanza that had eluded them in the gold fields of California, it was chickenfeed.

Times were tough for Orrum. Her husband had decided that having one wife simply wasn't enough, and as was his "right" under Mormon law, he took another. This new arrangement didn't sit well with the fiery Scottish girl. She promptly left Hunter for another prospector, a young man by the name of Cowan. She was about to leap from the frying pan into the fire.

Cowan was also a Mormon and although he decided that Allison was more than enough wife for any one man to handle, his religion still seemed to get in the way of marital bliss. At the time, the Mormon Church was considered "reactionary" by the United States Government and Federal troops were rumored on the way to quell the alleged "uprising." A decree came down from church leaders that all true Mormons must return immediately to Salt Lake and make preparations to defend the city. Newlywed Cowan, faithful to his religion if not his wife, obediently heeded the call.

Husbandless for the second time, Allison Orrum set up a boardinghouse to make ends meet and thanks to her Scottish knack for thrift and her old-fashioned home cooking (a rarity in the region), soon the establishment was thriving.

Among her boarders was a feisty young man named Sandy Bowers. Sandy had run up a sizeable hotel bill and, having little luck prospecting, the likelihood of settling his account was slim.

History doesn't record if it was love or financial gain that precipitated the relationship between Sandy Bowers and Allison Orrum, 14 years his senior. But the couple was eventually married in a solemn ceremony surrounded by well wishers. As a wedding present, Sandy gave his bride a small strip of land adjacent to claims that were "meager at best." But it was a beginning.

A lot of the diggings in Gold Canyon were turning out to be "meager" to say the least. As the months passed, more and more of the miners left looking for greener pastures. Many put up their claims at sale prices a fraction of their cost. On a hunch, Allison persuaded Sandy to buy them up.

Call it intuition, call it luck. No matter. Soon one of the richest strikes ever recorded was discovered on the "worthless" diggings. Almost overnight, Allison and Sandy Bowers were multi-millionaires. Only one small problem now remained: What to do with all the money?

The poor Scottish girl had but two grand wishes in her life, to build a luxurious mansion and to meet the Queen of England. Allison decided to kill two birds with one stone and soon the couple sailed for Great Britain. Upon arrival, she went on a shopping spree befitting her new-found wealth. She bought crystal chandeliers and priceless works of art. Fine French furniture, exotic marble statuary and lavish tapestries were ordered.

And all the while she waited anxiously for an audience with Queen Victoria.

But it was not to be. English morality at the time would not allow the Queen to receive a divorcee, no matter how rich. Allison and Sandy returned to the Comstock with enough furnishings to stock ten mansions, but she never met the Queen.

Soon that luxurious home began to take shape on the edge of Washoe Valley and, for its time, it was one of the finest anywhere in the west. But Sandy did not share his wife's desire for comfortable surroundings, preferring instead to spend time with his cronies from his prospecting days. He refused to live in the elegant mansion and shortly after it was completed, Sandy Bowers died. The young millionaire was but 35 years of age.

From there it was all downhill for his lady. The Bowers fortune was soon depleted by more lavish spending sprees and Allison was forced to sell the mansion. The new owner, a prominent businessman, took pity on her and offered her a job as a maid in her former household. But even that didn't last. Allison Orrum Bowers was fired. Penniless, she retired to Reno, where she read fortunes to make ends meet. She passed away a few years later.

But she left her mark indelibly on the Silver State. Bowers Mansion, today a popular tourist attraction, still remains, a legacy to a pretty Scottish girl who went from rags to riches...and back again.

NEVADA'S FIRST 'REAL' CHRISTMAS
-22-

Christmas in early Nevada was not the best of times. For many, it was perhaps the worst. For the mostly male population it was a time of sadness, of memories of friends long forgotten, of families far away. For most of the early prospectors, Christmas was a friendly whiskey bottle and a silent toast set to the mournful tickle of an out-of-tune upright piano.

Christmas dinner? It was not, certainly, the traditional fare, for meat of any kind was scarce. In the days before refrigeration, any meat to be had was driven to the table very much alive and butchered as the need arose. A succulent ham or a tender, juicy turkey for Christmas dinner? Out of the question. A scarcity of pork would not allow a hog to be butchered merely as a 'celebration' and there was not a single turkey anywhere in the state of Nevada.

Until, that is, the year 1866 rolled around.

His name was Hooker and he owned a hardware store in Hangtown, California. Today we know it as Placerville, but back then the original name was by far the more appropriate. It was a bustling, rambling frontier town still fired up in the aftermath of the nation's first gold rush.

Hooker's Hardware was doing a land office business. Shirts were selling for $10.00 each and what shovels could be had were bringing the princely sum of $15.00.

It was then that tragedy struck.

One night a disastrous fire destroyed the hardware store and Hooker, with little insurance, was left penniless. Fire was by far the most deadly opponent of frontier expansion and Hooker was devastated. He managed to salvage some of his inventory, but when it was sold, it brought but a measly $1,000.00.

But Hooker was certainly not a man to throw in the towel. While scouring the area for a new investment, he came upon an interesting piece of information. The California foothills had an abundant crop of turkeys that year. On the other side of the Sierra, however, in the isolated mining camps of Nevada, there were none. With the holidays just a few months away, turkeys, he reasoned, would bring top dollar from lonely miners resigned to dried venison, beans and sourdough. Here was a golden opportunity to regain his depleted fortune.

Of course, businessman Hooker still had one small problem. Drifts 15 feet high were already being reported in the Sierra making travel by any conveyance hazardous at best. With horses and mules having a rough go of it, how, he wondered, would he get a flock of turkeys through?

His plan was ingenious. If the best way to get beef to Washoe was on a cattle drive, why not, he thought, hold a "turkey" drive. It had never been tried before, but maybe, just maybe, it could work.

He immediately set his plan into motion. He hired two men with some trailherd experience. Next he bought two sheep dogs and set about training them to move the birds. In less than two weeks, he was ready. But a new storm was already moving into the Sierra.

The first few days were uneventful. But as they reached the western crest of the mountains, the drive was caught in the fury of a raging Nevada blizzard. As the freezing cold and gale-force winds descended on the party, the men dipped the turkey's feet in a mixture of tar and sand, then wrapped them in burlap for protection.

At one point, they came to a precarious dropoff. Prompted by the over-zealous sheep dogs, the turkeys took off into the wild blue yonder. It was almost a week before they could be rounded up.

It was one of the biggest gambles in history. Certainly, it seemed an impossible undertaking. But somehow Hooker and his turkeys made it.

They arrived in Carson City the week before Christmas and joyous miners snapped up his entire flock before nightfall on the very first day. Each man paid the incredible sum of $5.00. Each man thought the price miniscule.

Hooker himself made a small fortune from his wild endeavor, enough to retire to a ranch in Arizona where he spent the remainder of his days.

But perhaps the most important footnote to the story is this: On Christmas Day, 1866, turkey was served as a traditional meal for the very first time...

"Great day for items. I got through at 12 o'clock at night and wrote steadily all evening. We got a telegram this morning, announcing that the President has issued a proclamation making us a state. Hurrah for the State of Nevada!"

—Comstock journalist Alf Doten—
October 31, 1864

BUTCH CASSIDY
DID HE REALLY
ROB THE BANK?
-23-

Paul Newman played him in the movie. Robert Redford played his sidekick, the Sundance Kid. As we all know, ol' Butch was quite a fella, a born leader, a western Robin Hood. He pulled off Nevada's most famous bank robbery. Or did he..?

Today, Winnemucca, Nevada is a tranquil town. But around the turn of the century it was anything but. The rush to find more gold and silver after the decline of the Comstock Lode was followed by the coming of the railroad. Suddenly, Winnemucca, a mining and ranching center, became one of those rip-snortin', gun-totin' frontier towns that we all love to see in the movies.

On September 19, 1900, three men walked calmly into the First National Bank. They held the manager, George Nixon, at gunpoint, then walked out with more than $30,000 in gold.

As the men fled, they dropped one of the money sacks and gold spilled out all over the street. The robbery suddenly became a comedy of errors. Manager Nixon and a customer gave chase, emptying their handguns at the bandits. But not a single shot hit the mark. The men scrambled to their horses and rode off.

Soon the Deputy Sheriff was in hot pursuit. Fearing that the outlaws had too big a lead, he commandeered a freight train and after uncoupling the railroad cars, he gave the order to pour the coal to the engine.

But the robbers had planned the holdup well. While George Nixon was tending to his chores at the First National Bank, the outlaws had stolen some of Nixon's horses from his nearby ranch and hidden them in an arroyo. Changing mounts outside of town, they managed to outdistance the freight train and escape. They were never seen again.

The robbery became the stuff of which legends are made.

It was Butch Cassidy and the Hole in the Wall gang, the townsfolk said. It had to be. No one else could have pulled off such a daring robbery. And in broad daylight too. Operating under that vague premise, the bank hired the famous Pinkerton Detective Agency to embark on a nationwide manhunt. When the efforts of the detectives proved futile, the bank even signed bounty hunter Tom Horn (played by Steve McQueen in another famous western) to track them down. All to no avail. The rumors that Cassidy had outfoxed the greatest law enforcement agency in the country grew.

Just a few months later a photo arrived in the mail showing Butch, Sundance, Kid Curry and other members of the gang posing big as life in New York City. Dressed immaculately in dapper attire, they looked more like bank owners than bank robbers. More rumors began to circulate. It was Butch himself that had sent the picture, some said. He was deliberately poking fun at the hapless detectives bent on his capture. "They can get all the lawmen in the country, but they'll never get Butch," was the general consensus.

But was it *really* Butch Cassidy? Was it the Hole in the Wall gang that had robbed the bank in Winnemucca? Or were Butch and Sundance and their paramour Etta Place actually frolicking in South America as portrayed in the movie? What was fact? What was fiction?

The files of Wells Fargo and Company tell the tale. A Fargo detective, working undercover as a gambler, happened to spot a picture in the window of a photo gallery in Fort Worth, Texas. It showed a group of well-dressed, smug-looking men smiling for the photographer. Immediately recognizing some of the men, he forwarded the photograph on to the Pinkertons. They positively identified the men in the picture. It was Butch Cassidy and his gang, alright. Knowing about the search for Cassidy near Winnemucca, they slipped the photo in the mail anonymously to Nevada authorities. It made a great practical joke. That photograph, taken at another place and another time, became almost as famous as the robbery.

The holdup men were never caught. None of the gold was ever recovered. Eventually, however, the robbers were identified by Pinkerton agents as "hangers on" who probably, at one time or another, had ridden with Cassidy.

But Butch himself was never involved. Even banker Nixon, after studying the photograph at great length, stated positively that Butch Cassidy was not among the men who had walked into his bank that fateful day.

When Butch and Sundance were finally gunned down by Bolivian troops in South America, the Pinkertons officially abandoned the search and the case was closed. George Nixon left his bank and his Winnemucca ranch and moved to Tonopah. Eventually, he went on to become a United States Senator.

So despite what you've heard, it wasn't Butch who robbed that Winnemucca bank way back in 1900. Nonetheless, that robbery remains the most famous in Nevada history.

Did Butch Really Rob The Bank?

This photo of Butch Cassidy and the Hole in the Wall Gang was reportedly taken in New York City near the time of the robbery of the First National Bank in Winnemucca on September 19, 1900.

Jim Butler

Jim Butler, discoverer of Tonopah, poses with one of the burros that unearthed the fateful ledge.

Captain John

Many of Nevada's Indians were friendly, indeed helpful, to early white settlers. Although he looks warlike in this photograph, Captain John was anything but.

Ulysses S. Grant

Ulysses S. Grant, shown here fifth from the left, posed for photos along the fabulous Comstock.

Photograph courtesy of the Nevada Historical Society

At the time, Virginia City had more people than San Francisco

Almost overnight, a huge metropolis which boasted more than 30,000 people, sprung up on the slopes of Mt. Davidson. This early photo of Virginia City shows the tremendous influx of humanity.

Photograph courtesy of the Nevada Historical Society

Philip Deidesheimer

Without the creative genius of Philip Deidesheimer, most of Nevada's silver would have remained deep underground. Deidesheimer credited a honeybee for his ingenious design for square set mining.

The square set stope—
a revolutionary new technique for mining.

It is estimated that at any one time, fully one third of Virginia City's population worked underground, thanks to Philip Deidesheimer's new mining technique.

Rawhide

The town of Rawhide during the visit of famous author Elinor Glyn. Rawhide was one of the first Nevada settlements to utilize public relations people.

Frank Bell

Frank Bell made history by tapping out America's longest telegram.
The telegram consisted of the Nevada State Constitution in its
entirety. He would go on to become an early Nevada Governor.

Old Virginny

This rare photograph of James Finney, known affectionately as "Old Virginny," shows the style of the day. Finney lent his nickname to metropolis known as Virginia City.

Tourism Comes To Goldfield

Here the Gans—Nelson fight, forerunner of modern boxing exhibitions in Nevada, takes place in Goldfield.

Photograph courtesy of the Nevada Historical Society

Winnemucca

The bustling town of Winnemucca is shown here in the 1930's where Ohie McGillicutty suffered his bout of "alcoholoremia."

The second best writer on the Comstock.

This is an early photograph of Dan DeQuille who worked side by side with Mark Twain at the Territorial Enterprise in Virginia City.

Photograph courtesy of the Nevada Historical Society

He gave Mark Twain his big break.

Dennis McCarthy was editor of the Territorial Enterprise when Mark Twain was hired as a fledgling reporter.

Gold Hill or Slippery Gulch?

Although local residents referred to this bustling boomtown as Gold Hill, nearby rival Virginia City residents called the town Slippery Gulch. Refuse, including the carcasses of dead animals, constantly was washed down the middle of the street by spring runoff.

Photograph courtesy of the Nevada Historical Society

He kept his millions in Nevada.

John Mackay was the only one of the "Big Four" who kept his
fabulous silver wealth within the state.

Is this or is this not Mark Twain?

Some sources say this early photograph is the young Sam Clemens.

NICKANORA, THE SPANISH KING
-24-

He was dashing, a man-of-the-world, given to fancy dress and crisp, flamboyant speech. He entertained some of Nevada's most famous politicians at lavish dinner parties, serving them such rarities as pheasant under glass and imported French champagne served in solid silver chalices by liveried waiters.

His real name was Nickanor Rodrigues, but to most everyone on the Comstock, he was known simply as Nickanora. Born the son of a Spanish army officer, he spent his youth in old California. By age 16, he was captured robbing a stagecoach in Tuolumne County and sentenced to 10 years in prison. After serving only a few months, he was released because of his tender age.

For the next several years, he drifted through the gold fields of northern California, running for a time, rumor said, with the famous outlaw Joaquin Murietta. By the time he reached the Comstock at the height of the silver booms, young Rodrigues headed his own small band of Mexican outlaws. They were about to become fabulously rich.

Their first robbery didn't even require guns. Nickanora simply took a job as a foreman at the Imperial Mill in Gold Hill. As the mill was hardly ever watched, Nickanora deftly snatched molten silver amalgam out of the retorts, right under the eye of the superintendent. It has been estimated that over a seven-month period, the gang managed to relieve the milling operation of more than $800,000 in ore. And all the time, Nickanora and several of his men were pulling down paychecks as well. The mill owners never suspected the wily Mexican.

Now wealthy, the man who was becoming known as "The Spanish King" found work no longer to his liking. He had discovered gold, he said, and his "claim" had proved to be a rich one.

He was now a man of leisure. He began to roam the streets of Virginia City, constantly on the alert for what he openly referred to as "new investments."

They were soon in coming. One afternoon, he filled a wheelbarrow with unretorted bullion at the Pacific Mill and, in broad daylight, walked off with it.

On another occasion he spotted three bars of pure silver from the Ophir Mine being loaded aboard a Wells Fargo stage bound for nearby Reno. Nickanora hastily bought a ticket and brazenly mounted the coach, plunking himself down right next to the driver, Baldy Green.

By the time the coach had reached the valley floor, darkness had fallen, and somewhere between Steamboat Springs and the Reno city limits, he distracted Green and pitched the bars of bullion off into a ditch. In Reno, he hired a buggy and doubled back over the route to recover the silver.

Naturally the theft was quickly discovered. At first light a Washoe County constable rode back toward Steamboat and found the tracks of a buggy that had suddenly become extremely heavy. He followed the tracks right up to the door of a Slippery Gulch assay office where he learned that a "handsome Mexican businessman" had left them there with instructions to "melt them down and recast them in smaller bars."

Upon learning of the constable's visit, Nickanora never returned for his silver bars. He just went on to bigger and better things.

Over the next several years, hardly a stagecoach or mudwagon was safe on the Comstock. At one point, Wells Fargo and Company became so frustrated with their inability to catch red-handed the bandit they knew full well was responsible that they offered him a "job" instead. Under cover of darkness, Colonel W.W. Bishop, an attorney for the stageline, left Pioche and rode to the base of Spring Mountain where Nickanora was rumored to be hiding. There he offered the Mexican $2,000.00 a month. The bandit was free to pursue his vocation as long as he did not touch any of the stages belonging to Wells Fargo. The outlaw accepted the proposal.

For a time the agreement was profitable for both parties. True to his word, the coaches and freight wagons of Wells Fargo were never touched. Wells Fargo, now being touted as "the safest way to traverse the mountains," saw its cargo volume steadily increase.

But, as luck would have it, one day there was a change in management at Wells and Fargo and into the office of the superintendent walked Nickanora. Sizing up the new manager, a man named Siebert, he politely quipped, "I am extremely regretful, Senor, but my agreement was with your predecessor and not with you. You must make your own arrangements to protect your property." The startled Siebert declined.

Whether it was some strange outlaw code of ethics or a slow realization that he could make much more than $2,000.00 a month if he concentrated his interest on Wells Fargo, no one can be sure. But soon Wells Fargo coaches were again being robbed on a regular basis.

Finally, his fabulous run of good luck ran out. After an exhaustive investigation involving almost every peace officer within 4 counties, Nickanora was captured and sentenced to prison without the possibility of parole. Within a year, he and two others broke out of jail and fled across the border to a ranch on the Sevier River in Utah. After taking fresh horses from the ranch of C.H. Light, they headed south toward Mexico. A posse, which had been gradually gaining on them, found two bodies. They were Nickanora's two companions, shot to death. Nickanora himself had simply vanished.

Years later, a man calling himself Don Felipe Castro Estrada, the wealthy owner of a sprawling rancho in the mountains of northern Mexico, was supposedly identified as the famous bandit, but no attempts were ever made to prove the validity of the allegations.

To this day, the legend exists. Of Nickanora, the Spanish King, who, for a time, was the most famous outlaw in the silver state.

"I am not into speculating in the stock market. My business is mining, legitimate mining. I see that my men do their work properly and all goes well as it should in the mines. I make my money here out of the ore.

"Naturally, if I had a desire to do so, I could go down to San Francisco with 10,000 shares of stock in my pocket and by throwing it on the market at the critical moment, I could bring about a panic. But suppose I did that and made half a million by the job -what is that to me? But attending to my legitimate business here in Nevada, I can take that much out within a week.

—John Mackey—
Mining baron

THE ENTERPRISE THE MOST FAMOUS PAPER IN THE WEST
-25-

In its heydey, its payroll boasted the names of some of the finest writers in the country -men like Mark Twain, Dan DeQuille, Sam Davis, Rollin Daggett and Art McEwen. It was blunt, candid, outrageous, free-spirited and, sometimes, downright mean. At one time, its daily circulation was more than 15,000, making it the largest newspaper west of the Mississippi. It was, of course, the famous Territorial Enterprise.

It was 1858 when a man named Jernegan and his partner Alfred James founded the Enterprise in the Mormon settlement of Genoa. At the time, most of Nevada was known simply as Carson County, Utah Territory, and the newspaper business was far from brisk. The great silver strikes were still a few years away and news at the time was usually limited to stories of land acquisitions and eastern items, most of the news brought by passing settlers and, inherently, months old.

Meanwhile, in nearby Carson City, business was booming. The fact that the city was rapidly becoming a regional freight center provided more than enough material to fill a tabloid. The fledgling editors packed up their paper and moved to Carson.

But soon disaster struck. It was rumored that Jernegan was simply a poor business manager. Regardless, the publication suddenly found itself on the verge of bankruptcy. After a violent argument, the men split up, Jernegan cursing his partner, his paper and the territory all at the same time. "I call on God to curse the Enterprise," Jernegan wrote in his diary, "and all, dead or alive, who robbed me!"

Fortunately God didn't happen to be listening. James moved the Enterprise again, this time to a small mining town at the foot of Mount Davidson, Virginia City. The year was 1860.

Perhaps the curse came true; perhaps he simply tired of the business. But soon Al James decided to sell the paper. It wound up in the hands of a second set of partners, Joe Goodman and Dennis McCarthy, who were not only newspapermen but also men who happened to be in the right place at the right time. Scraping together just a few hundred dollars, they took over the reins of the faltering Enterprise. Little did they know that Virginia City was about to become the biggest city in the west, with more than 30,000 people. And almost every single one of them was a raucous, rambunctious newsmaker.

The subsequent success of the Enterprise would be considered phenomenal even today. Goodman and McCarthy conducted business on a cash-and-carry basis and for a time, the paper was netting an incredible $1,000.00 a day. The partners, it was rumored, carried the cash home each night in a water bucket.

The popularity of the Territorial Enterprise was due in part to the uncanny poetic license afforded its writers. In the day before copy readers, reporters simply wrote what they pleased (indeed, it was common practice to 'make up' stories on slow news days) and simply hung the copy on "the hook." The printer set type exactly as written and printed it that way.

The unprecedented creative freedom paid off handsomely. DeQuille, for example, once made up a tale about some magic rocks. He called his creation "The Traveling Stones of Paranagatt Valley," and in the story he boasted that he had discovered some strange rocks that could "move around quite freely by themselves." Though total fiction, the story wound up all the way on the east coast where it was printed as gospel. Promoter P.T. Barnum, a hoaxer himself, was completely taken in. He offered DeQuille $10,000.00 for his "traveling stones." DeQuille, who knew his rocks were merely magnetic and quite common in the Paranagatt Valley, honorably declined.

Such freedom of expression was, at times, a double-edged sword. Many an Enterprise writer, Mark Twain included, had his eyes blackened by disgruntled readers who objected to stories written about them. DeQuille was challenged to a shootout, not once but twice.

Despite its unprecedented success, the Enterprise lasted only as long as the Comstock Lode. In January of 1893, it published its last edition. Leading newspapers across the country printed stirring sympathetic obituaries for the Enterprise. Even the prestigious Society of Pacific Coast Pioneers flew its flag at half mast.

The Territorial Enterprise went out quietly, without a whine or a whimper. Its final editorial stated simply, "For sufficient reason, we stop."

Since that time, attempts have been made to restore the newspaper to its former glory, and, given the increase in tourism, the Enterprise may once again make a glorious comeback.

But the going will be tough. Sadly, Virginia City's population no longer numbers in the thousands, but in the hundreds...

DAN DE QUILLE
THE SECOND BEST WRITER
ON THE COMSTOCK
-26-

Everybody's heard of Mark Twain. From his humble beginnings on the staff of the Territorial Enterprise, he went on to fame and fortune as one of America's most beloved storytellers. But sharing the reporting duties on the Enterprise was another man, Dan DeQuille, who, although he was destined to play second fiddle to Twain, was considered by many to be a far better writer.

His real name was William Wright, but like most reporters on the frontier, he wrote under a nom de plume.

It was not because of wit or style, or even ego. It was a matter of safety, plain and simple. It was common practice, not only in Virginia City, but in other boomtowns on the frontier, to "beat on the editor," literally to contest the writing of a particular story with fist, knife or whatever happened to be handy. Desecration being the better part of valor, most writers chose to write factitiously, thus saving themselves from bodily harm.

But DeQuille was not of this ilk. He was a shy man, well-liked on the Comstock, highly respected by the Bonanza kings and amazingly well versed in mining. So great was his mining expertise that one day he astounded magnates John Mackay and Jim Fair by casually mentioning what they considered their best-kept secret, the location of a new body of ore deep underground. DeQuille, without setting foot inside the shaft, had deduced its location simply from his study of mineralogy.

Mining was his first and perhaps only love. He would rather report on the latest results at the Belcher, the Lady Bryan or the Ophir Mine than cover the latest presidential election. The shootouts, hangings, and fist fights, he usually left to Twain.

Regardless of his scientific bent, he was not a man to be sneezed at in the practical joke department. Like Twain, when he found a day becoming a little "light in the news department," he often just made some news stories up —as in the case of his report of the magnetic stones.

For example, he wrote of a "revolutionary new device" which would allow prospectors to work for days out in the middle of the desert without so much as a "trickle of sweat." The device consisted of a helmet and a suit, wrote DeQuille, which contained small amounts of ammonia. As the substance evaporated, he claimed, it gave off a "cool breeze" which kept the prospector fresh for days on end despite the blistering 110 degree heat.

Not content to stop there, he wrote of an experiment that had been conducted to prove the invention's reliability. He reported that a miner testing the device had not returned from the desert. Two days later he wrote that a search party had been sent into action. The entire population of Virginia City waited the results with baited breath.

Then he administered the coup de grace. A blaring headline appeared proclaiming that the miner had been found, frozen to death! Frozen stiff in the middle of the desert! DeQuille asserted that the poor fellow had released too much ammonia and had been transformed into a human ice cube. Though the story had sprung unfettered from DeQuille's fertile imagination, it was picked up by none other than the prestigious London Times which printed its own version detailing the "solar armor experiments" which were being conducted in primitive Nevada.

Despite his great writing skills, fortune would always elude Dan DeQuille. For more than 40 years he continued to work as a reporter for the Enterprise, taking time off only once to write a definitive history of the Comstock, *The Big Bonanza*. Sadly, it was a financial disaster. He returned to his $60.00 a month salary at the newspaper. But he never seemed to mind. Even when the fabulous Comstock Lode eventually petered out, he showed little emotion, though the Enterprise folded and left him without a penny.

Still, he was not destined to die a pauper. His close friend of many years, multi-millionaire miner John Mackay, learned that in the interim DeQuille had left town. He instructed his secretary to "find Dan, pay off any debts that he may have, buy him two of the finest suits this town has to offer and then employ a companion to accompany him to his place of birth in Iowa." It was done.

And even after DeQuille left Virginia City had returned to what he had always called "the states," he continued to receive support from Mackay. Until his death several years later, a draft arrived each month in the sum of $60.00, the exact amount of his former salary at the Enterprise.

Joe Goodman, DeQuille's flamboyant boss for many years and the man who had hired both he and Mark Twain, said sadly, "Isn't it so singular that Mark Twain should live and Dan DeQuille fade out? If anyone had asked me in 1863 which would have been the immortal name, I should unhesitatingly have said Dan DeQuille. Fate, it seems," wrote Goodman, "rewards audacity."

"Virginia City now lies stricken and old. The mountainside which shook and echoed with the stamps of a score of mills is silent. A few of the old timers linger on, a C Street sign seeks pathetically to keep up the show despite the grim, staring ruins of the old Wells Fargo Building. The churches alone stand staunch and unshaken.

"Above, on the slopes of Mount Davidson, are rows of ramshackle wooden buildings, some of them four stories high, leaning against each other in desolate insecurity. A Washoe zephyr might huff and puff and blow them down like a house of cards. Most of the houses which clung to the slopes in this fair city were torn down long ago, often board by board and used for firewood. Tis sad indeed. So passes the glory of the Comstock...

—Editor Wells Drury—
Describing the town in the 1880'S

MARK TWAIN AND
THE PROSPECTING PIG
-27-

They were fast friends, Jim Gillis and Samuel Langhorne Clemens. They had met when Clemens was still working as a miner, hacking away at a small claim down around Aurora way and barely managing to make ends meet. The fortunes of both men, however, began to turn around when they finally hit raucous and rowdy Virginia City.

Those were fabulous times, the 1860's. The Comstock Lode was a rich, almost mystical body of ore that many thought would never end. Jim Gillis continued prospecting. His partner went to work for the Territorial Enterprise, eventually taking the pen name Mark Twain. Resettlement in Virginia City would prove to be a profitable move for both.

The two men were story-tellers of the first order. Often they would spend quiet evenings together, swapping tall tales that later would become the subjects of many of Twain's writings.

Although it was Twain who was renowned for ready wit and wisdom, Gillis was a man of infinite ingenuity as well. He had taken to pocket mining and was reasonably successful. (For the uninitiated, this type of mining involves a lot of leg work. You scour the countryside searching for hidden crevices, or 'pockets' containing gold.)

Naturally, this type of labor left a lot to be desired. After all, it's no fun hiking up and down a mountainside with a pick over your shoulder. So Gillis decided to get himself some help. He bought a pig. That's right, a pig! And he trained the porker to do his prospecting for him.

First, he baked some biscuits. You see, John Henry, the pig, was very fond of biscuits. Next, he buried them up and down the slope near his isolated cabin. Summoning John Henry, the wily Gillis again headed up the canyon and began to dig. Whenever he uncovered one of the biscuits, he fed it to John Henry. Needless to say, the pig was delighted with the 'discovery.' For days, Jim Gillis kept up the pig's training —burying biscuits, then digging them up again. John Henry loved every minute of it. Pigs are pretty smart, so it wasn't long before John Henry caught on. Soon every time Gillis set out with pick in hand, John Henry would let out a squeal and take off ahead of him, ripping up the ground like a deranged ditch digger. As a result, Gillis merely had to follow along, casually searching for color. It was prospecting the lazy man's way, but it worked. In this fashion, Gillis found a considerable amount of gold.

But I was digressing. I was planning to tell you how John Henry would figure prominently in the fortunes of Mark Twain...

Jim Gillis's cabin had four bunks, a rarity in Virginia City. One he occupied himself, two were used by other men with whom he shared the housekeeping chores and the fourth was vacant. Here's where the plot thickens...

In addition to the pig, Gillis also had a bulldog, a tenacious little fella named Towser. The pug and the pig were fond of wrestling with each other and occasionally, on cold winter nights, Gillis would let them into the cabin. Once inside, they would make a mad dash for the empty bed and playfully thrash around on it until they fell asleep. It was all great fun. Until, one evening, along came Mark Twain.

As was their custom, Twain and Gillis spent the evening swapping stories, talking long into the night. As dawn approached, Twain decided to stay over and Gillis, always the practical joker, offered the empty bunk.

When Twain was fast asleep, Gillis slipped quietly from his cot and opened the front door. Sure enough, in rushed John Henry and Towser who immediately leapt into their favorite bunk. Twain, caught in his bedroll, was trapped. The dog and the pig proceeded to wrestle about, playing havoc while Twain screamed for mercy.

Jim Gillis, laughing hysterically, eventually managed to pull the dog and pig off their helpless victim, but Twain was furious. He called his friend just about every name in the book and then some. He threatened murder and mayhem. He vowed never again to darken Jim Gillis's door. Only when Gillis agree to tell him "the most incredible story you've ever heard," did he calm down.

Together, the two men ushered the animals outdoors, uncorked another whiskey bottle, and Gillis began.

The story? Believe it or not, it turned out to be the "Celebrated Jumping Frog of Calaveras County," the yarn that would become one of Twain's first true literary successes. Mark Twain would go on to become the nation's most popular humorist and wealthy beyond his wildest dreams.

Fate works in mysterious ways. Perhaps Mark Twain would never have gone on to greatness without the help of a pig named John Henry, a dog named Towser and a practical-joking prospector by the name of Jim Gillis.

THE BANSHEE OF ESMERALDA
-28-

The Esmeralda range was hardly true to its name. Although the region yielded more than its share of gold and silver, most of the claims were small. But the area did boast something else, a banshee, that sullen ghost that shows itself on the eve of an impending death.

Patrick Murphy was, in the words of his friends, "a fine old Irish gentlemen." He prospected when the spirit moved him, doing reasonably well at the task and he maintained a well-kept ranch and vegetable garden which made him a particular favorite of passersby.

His ranch was located in an isolated canyon just a few short miles from Whiskey Flat. Murphy, though an affable fellow, preferred to live alone. His only companion was another Irishman, Jeremiah Degin, who helped him at odd jobs from time to time.

It was late in October, 1871. Darkness had fallen as the two men returned to their cabin. Suddenly, there, on the rim of the canyon, they spotted an eerie glow. Moving closer, they saw the apparition rise, slowly at first. As the men watched in horror, the form began to expand, then contract. The miners beat a hasty retreat to the safety of their cabin.

Superstition had gotten the best of them. "Tis a banshee, sure!" said Murphy. "I know I shall die before the sun comes up!" His companion Degin was equally convinced that it would be he, not Murphy, who was about to meet his Maker. With the door tightly bolted, the men huddled together to await the inevitable.

But as dawn approached, they began to feel much better. They were certainly alive. Their courage now bolstered, they returned to the spot where the 'banshee' had appeared. They found not a trace of the would-be ghost.

But the next night, there it was again, a mysterious form

hovering against the canyon wall. For the second night in a row, the men cringed behind locked doors. The following morning, although they were still alive, they rode into Whiskey Flat and had their wills prepared.

It was then that a Jewish peddler, Soloman Sloan, happened by. He'd heard the wild tales of the banshee and decided to see for himself. Lantern at the ready, Sloan joined the terrified prospectors behind a jagged outcropping as darkness descended.

Sure enough, the 'ghost' appeared. But far from frightened, Sloan just hefted his lantern and approached the figure. Murphy and Degin watched as Sloan's lantern came within inches of the 'banshee.' Suddenly, both lights went out. Murphy and Degin fled.

Within a few minutes, Sloan knocked on their cabin door. His lantern had been blown out by the wind, he explained. The apparition? It was hardly a banshee, said Sloan. It was simply a cavity of phosphorescent rock. When the moonlight and the temperature were just right, he told the frightened men, it glowed in the dark. He convinced the pair to return with him to the spot. Sure enough, the banshee of Esmeralda had disappeared.

But Sloan himself disappeared as well. There was no trace of him in Whiskey Flat for days. Since he had last been spotted on his way to the Murphy ranch, the authorities rode to the ranch and, suspecting foul play, promptly arrested the prospectors.

But their jail term was brief. It was learned that Sloan had sold his wagon and all his belongings in nearby Dayton, saying he was tired of his itinerant lifestyle and was "off to greener pastures." The sheriff, embarrassed by his over-zealousness, released the men with a public apology.

Two years passed.

One afternoon a traveler appeared in Whiskey Flat with a New York newspaper under his arm. As was the custom, the paper was passed from hand to hand as the residents of the isolated community poured hungrily over the news from the east.

There it was —a short paragraph at the bottom of the second page. It told of one Solomon Sloan who had just consummated an extraordinary sale. The account suggested that in his western travels, Sloan "has come into the possession of one of the largest diamonds ever unearthed." It told how the peddler had just completed the sale of his gem to the Ambassador from Russia. It would become a gift to the Russian Czar.

Murphy was stunned. Then enraged. His mind flashed back to that night in the canyon when Sloan had brazenly confronted the banshee. The 'ghost' had never been seen again despite the fact that the moonlight and the temperatures had been identical on many other occasions. Murphy was convinced that it had been a diamond, not some eerie phosphorescent, that had given off that glow. He was suddenly convinced that he had been hoodwinked by the drummer, that Sloan had simply pocketed the diamond and skipped town.

Of course, whether Sloan's diamond actually came from that canyon on the outskirts of Whiskey Flat, no one ever knew. But one thing was certain: Diamond or no diamond, a poor peddler from Nevada had suddenly become very rich. And the Banshee of the Esmeralda has never been seen since...

"Reno is dull because its roots -socially, humanly speaking -are fastened in decay. If you like to put it that way, Reno is sinister. This little town with its girdle of enchanting mountains, its wide, well-kept streets, its delightful park where the Truckee River flows -irrigation creating for it a dense greenness in the midst of the hopeless desert -has a fairly equivocal future. Its past is the past of the great mining camps. It was bred in their tradition.

"The Reno magnates are men who knew and took their part in the earlier hectic days -sinking into old age and death now, squandering or saving their 'piles', but without any prospect of more 'piles' to be made. The gold and silver, you see, have gone. Even the Comstock Lode has petered out.

"It must never be forgotten that the human habit of Reno are the tradition, the point of view, the human habit of a mining camp. A mining camp after the gold is gone is not a colorful or an exciting place. The big men, the great adventurers, go and only the little men and the habit of gambling for lessening stakes are left...

—Author Katherine Geroald—
1925

MILT SHARP
NEVADA'S MOST
NOTORIOUS HIGHWAYMAN
-29-

"He was one of the politest gentlemen I ever met," said one fellow back in June of 1880. It was a pretty amazing admission. Especially when you consider that the man to whom he had been referring had just robbed him of all his worldly possessions.

Milton Anthony Sharp was his name, and of all the bandits that laid claim to the possessions of Wells and Fargo, none was ever more notorious; none ever received such publicity. It was said that the main reason most of the gold that left Bodie never made it to the Carson City Mint was because of the notorious Milt Sharp.

His uncanny ability to pull off daring daylight holdups was hardly his only claim to fame. He became known as the "Polite Bandit," a man who would go out of his way to avoid violence and would even thank his victims before departing the scene.

That particular day in 1880, Sharp stopped a stage heading up grade from Carson City some 18 miles north of Wellington's, a wayside tavern. There, he politely asked the passengers, including the driver, Tom Chamberlain, to dismount and stand in a line with their backs to the coach. With everyone in place, he climbed up on the seat and broke open the strongbox. Climbing back down, he asked the passengers to empty their pockets and take three paces forward. As they complied, he scooped up their valuables. Apologizing profusely to his victims, he disappeared into the sagebrush.

Said one old timer who had been aboard the coach, "This stage robbing is a very nice business when artistically conducted and I've never seen anyone who could do it better than Milt Sharp!" High praise indeed for a highwayman.

Sharp continued to foil all attempts at his capture by Wells Fargo detectives. Instead of lighting out immediately after a robbery, he would often return to the very same spot and hold up the very same stagecoach. Just two weeks after the aforementioned robbery, Sharp appeared again and after separating Tom Chamberlain from the strongbox, he said cheerfully, "I am most sorrowful that I had to relieve you of your gold watch last time around." With a wink, he returned the timepiece to the startled driver.

It was his brazen attitude and uncanny ability to be in the right place at the right time that eventually led to the downfall of Milt Sharp. J.B. Hume, a Wells Fargo detective, figured that Sharp had to be a "California bandit" who had wandered over into Nevada to take advantage of the silver strikes. After all, Hume reasoned, the man was just too good. He sure hadn't gotten that experienced in fledgling Nevada.

On a hunch, Hume took off for San Francisco, where he staked out all the railway depots. Sure enough, within just a few days, a bag was found with the name Milton A. Sharp boldly stitched to the flap. When the bag was claimed, Hume arrested Milt Sharp. When the bag was opened, the spoils from several recent Nevada robberies were discovered. Milt Sharp, the polite bandit, was taken in irons back to Aurora for trial.

But the story doesn't end there. Within a week, with the help of an unknown accomplice, Sharp managed to remove some bricks from the wall of his jail cell and escaped into the wintry night. It was bitter cold and although he had been shackled with an Oregon Boot, a 15-pound iron shoe, no trace of the outlaw could be found.

By this time, however, Wells and Fargo had learned their lesson. Instead of sending out a posse in search of the wily Sharp, they sent a message out instead. They made it known that "until Sharp is in custody, Wells, Fargo and Company will carry nothing of value on their coaches."

Days became weeks and still there was no trace of Milt Sharp. The weather turned even colder. At night, temperatures dropped to more than 20 below. Some lawmen were thinking that perhaps Sharp had perished in the freezing desert.

One night a breathless miner stumbled into Donohue's Saloon calling for the sheriff. A man, he explained, was waiting on the outskirts of town to see him. When authorities arrived at the city limits, they found Milton Sharp. Nevada's most famous bandit, frozen, near starving and collapse, gave up without a fight.

Milt Sharp was eventually sentenced to 20 years in the Nevada State penitentiary.

The legend had come to an end.

When officers asked him why he had not held up a store or broken into some lonely miner's cabin for food and shelter, he replied, "I am a stage robber, sir. I would never stoop to burglary. Never in a hundred years!"

APRIL FOOL!
-30-

I miss April Fool's Day. It's just not as much fun as it used to be. When I was a kid, a scant 40 years ago, people stayed up nights dreaming up jokes that would have folks talking for years.

Not any more. Today, the local morning disc jockey might read a tongue-in-cheek headline or two but that's about it.

But back in the early days of Nevada's statehood, April Fool's Day was a genuine cause for celebration. Miners and prospectors had little to laugh at in those precarious times, so no excuse for merriment was ever overlooked. Particularly on April First.

I offer as proof the following April Fool's pranks that were perpetrated during Nevada's infancy, jokes both devious in their creation and masterful in implementation.

DAYTON - folks in town were awakened on that fateful morning by the passing of a solemn funeral procession. There was a brass band, a group of military drummers, and a coffin draped in black. When curious onlookers inquired as to the name of the deceased, they were told that the mayor, a most popular fellow, had passed away during the night.

Soon the news spread as eager reporters converged on the graveyard to cover the somber entombment. When the coffin was lowered into the ground, the lid popped open and out stepped the mayor, very much alive. The burial party then retired to the local saloon where his honor set up drinks for the house.

AUSTIN - A newspaper headline on April 1 boasted of a new silver strike, not in Nevada, but in California. Every horse and wagon had been rented from the livery stable and a boisterous crowd was already streaming out of town before the editor finally came clean. It was all a hoax.

PALISADE - A trainload of Easterners was greeted by the sound of gunfire. Rushing to the windows, the 'tenderfeet' witnessed a terrible gunfight. Two men were blasted by a shotgun right under the windows of the train. Four more fell 'dead' in the street as they tried to escape the hail of bullets. One man managed to stumble up into the main passenger coach and after 'bleeding' profusely on half the startled passengers, he 'died' in the arms of a pretty young woman who fainted dead away from all the excitement. The gunfight had been staged by rowdies from a local saloon.

VIRGINIA CITY - A poster was circulated advertising "Gustofus, the European Drinking Champion!" who claimed he could drink 6 kegs of beer at a single sitting. Several saloons provided the beverage and a huge crowd had gathered to witness the extraordinary event. "Gustofus" turned out to be a local miner with a terrible thirst, but without the wherewithal to quench it. He passed out after drinking a mere half keg. Although the townsfolk were miffed at the miner, they soon got over it. The remainder of the beer was consumed by onlookers and a good time was had by all.

AURORA - A band of Indians, lances high and warbonnets trailing in the wind, swept into town in the wee small hours of the morning, whooping it up at the top of their lungs. No one gave much thought to the date as the town battened down the hatches and men with rifles took to the rooftops. It was only when one of the "Indians" fell from his horse in a drunken stupor did the citizens realize that the "Redskins" were actually locals dressed in feathers and warpaint.

GOLD HILL - Residents awoke to find a tent show of unusual interest had opened at the edge of town. The featured attraction was "Fatima, the Sultan's Favorite! Direct from the wind-swept deserts of the exotic Far East!" Though tent shows were common at the time, this one garnered more than the usual share of attention. It was rumored that Fatima would appear completely nude, something unheard of in those days. By 10 a.m., tickets for the afternoon show had been sold out. Those that had purchased seats earlier for the $1.00 asking price refused to part with them, although offers of up to $100.00 were made.

At show time, the curtain rose to reveal the beautiful Fatima. She was every bit as lovely as the circulars had proclaimed. For the better part of an hour she paraded in front of the anxious crowd, teasing them with her belly dancing and erotic gestures. More than

200 raucous miners were primed to fever pitch. Then, with a flourish, Fatima disappeared behind a portable screen.

As the men waited breathlessly, pieces of her wardrobe flew high in the air. First her slippers and golden chains appeared, followed by several silken scarves. Next came her billowy harem pants, finally some brief undergarments. The crowd cheered wildly and the tension rose. Obviously Fatima was now naked, a first on the fabulous Comstock.

Two burly miners stepped up on to the stage and withdrew the screen. There, naked as the day she was born was —not the lovely Fatima (She had slipped out the back) but Maggie, a 5-foot tall, 230-pound madam from the red light district. It had all been one colossal practical joke.

Yep. I truly miss the April Fool's Days we used to have. Today something is missing from the celebration. Perhaps its our sense of humor, dulled into submission by the evening news and worldwide murder and mayhem. Say I, "Bring back the good ol' days!"

Now if I were a practical joker myself, I should finish this chapter with a joke of my own. For example, I could tell you that the highjinx you've been reading about never really happened at all.

Of course, I wouldn't do that to you. Or would I....

"Towns soon became ghost towns. The stores of Reno gave up their luxury lines. Show windows which once contained furs and silks for the New York trade began showing overalls and simple frocks again. Even the women who launched the crusade suffered. Ironically, many of their own husbands are now out of a job.

—Author Max Miller—
Upon the increase in the waiting period for a Nevada divorce. It was changed from 6 months to 1 year in 1913.

THE NEWSPAPER
THAT NEVER WAS
-31-

If you study some of Nevada's history as I do, you'll come to the conclusion that in the area of tall tales, this state plays second fiddle to none. In fact, tall tales are more abundant than sagebrush. Recreational lying occupies an honored place among our favorite pastimes. Witness the Sezerac Lying Club of old Austin. But for sheer audacity, it's doubtful anyone can top the story of the Wabuska Mangler, the phantom newspaper that never was.

Old time reporters will tell you that often they have a recurring nightmare. "Gee, what if nothing happens?" In other words, how do you fill a newspaper or a half-hour evening news program if nothing went on that day? Thanks to the help of electronic news services, we seldom have this problem in this day and age. But the Carson Appeal, the premier publication of our State Capitol back in the 1880's, wasn't quite so lucky.

You see, there had been plenty of news for a long, long time. There had been a silver strike just 30 years before and it had fired the imagination of the entire world. Politicians, financiers and railroad men, outlaws, opera singers and entrepreneurs had all converged on the Comstock with a vengeance and for decades they made for great copy.

As one reporter wrote at the time, "There is hardly a day that passes when there is not a shootout or a fistfight of some sort. I never seem to want for news in this amazing day and age. Happy am I to live in these most exciting of times." Yep, there were plenty of things happening in Nevada and local newspapers provided the blow-by-blow description.

But by 1880, things had calmed down a bit. Not only were shootouts and fistfights becoming a thing of the past, but not even the politicians were stepping out of line. Peace and quiet was becoming the rule in Carson City, not the exception, and that meant death for the Carson Appeal. What they needed was a promotion of some kind, a gimmick, something to perk the public interest and get folks reading again. Something....like a nice juicy feud.

It wasn't long before the people of Carson City were being treated to blaring headlines announcing in no uncertain terms an all-out attack on the editorial policies of the "scurrilous, lying, no-account, good-for-nothing fish wrapper, the Wabuska Mangler," and the "mean, vile, low-down skunk" who called himself its editor. The paper was published in far off Lyon County, by a man "so depraved that he would set his own grandmother's petticoats afire with her still in them!" The Mangler, wrote the Appeal, was "a rag," a "stain on the sacred profession of journalism."

What few people realized was that the Wabuska Mangler and its editor did not exist.

This kind of journalistic license was quite common on the frontier. "Making up" the news was practically an everyday occurrence. In the case of the Wabuska Mangler, the "news" was another newspaper.

The feud between the Carson Appeal and its factitious competitor heated up. The Appeal declared itself the savior of "pure, unsullied journalism" and warned people to avoid reading the Mangler at all costs. If readers of the story had their interest peaked, the Appeal wasn't worried in the least. It would be pretty hard to find a copy of a newspaper that didn't exist.

The smear campaign continued. When a popular cause arose, Carson City learned that the Wabuska Mangler was against it. When a badman was jailed it was reported that he had been labeled "a fine, upstanding citizen" by the Mangler. The Mangler's stories were always "erroneous" and "misleading" while the Appeal carried high the standard of "honesty and truth." It was totally unprofessional, absolutely unethical, but it was also hilarious. And, it sold a lot of Carson City newspapers.

But all good things, even the greatest of practical jokes, must come to an end. One day the Appeal reported that the editor of the Mangler had fled the country. Although it carefully avoided giving any specific details, the Carson paper hinted broadly that its rival had finally run afoul of the law and had left Nevada to avoid prosecution. The attacks on the Wabuska Mangler promptly ceased.

No one today is sure of the reason. Perhaps it was nothing more than a case of creative exhaustion by the staff of the Appeal. Perhaps the campaign had accomplished its goal of increased circulation. Nonetheless, the Mangler faded into the yellowing pages of history and was never heard from again.

But while it lasted, the imaginary Wabuska Mangler had become one of the biggest and best "tall tales" of all.

IN OLD VIRGINIA, IT WAS TOUGH TO FIND A JURY...
-32-

Storey County's first sheriff, W.H. Howard, didn't have much trouble finding a jury. After all, it was a murder trial and nothing, mused the lawman, fascinated decent folks quite as much as a nice juicy murder. And Howard was more than just interested. It was his first big trial and even though the murders had been committed long before he had been sworn in as sheriff, he wanted things to go right.

The crime itself had been gathering dust, so to speak. The two bodies had been found more than 2 years before, but there had been no clues to the identity of the killer or killers.

It had been so long ago. A man named Hancock had been traveling west with his wife and child when their wagon broke down. Two Good Samaritans, Billy Edmondson and 'Doc' Engstrom, had come along and offered to help. That night, after the wagon was repaired, the men retired to a welcome bedroll. They would never awaken. Days later, their mutilated bodies were discovered.

It would eventually come to light that during that fateful night, Hancock had killed the two men as they slept. At dawn, he commandeered their outfit and, removing all traces of his presence, headed on to California. His wife had kept quiet about the murders. Until now.

History does not record why she had waited so long, nor why she had even decided to cooperate at all. Just the same, Mrs. Hancock finally reported the grisly murders and her husband was brought back to Nevada for the trial.

Sheriff Howard gathered his jury without difficulty. After all, this trial was news. The defendant Hancock was a learned man, and the crime, though now years old, still seemed horrifying. Prospective jurors literally lined up for a chance to be in on the action.

The trial lasted only a few days. Faced with the damning testimony of his own wife, Hancock was soon found guilty and sentenced to be hung. Gracious even to the end, the condemned man solemnly addressed the jury, "Gentlemen, I thank you." Just as graciously, the foreman replied, "You, sir, are entirely welcome." With considerable ceremony, the convicted Hancock was marched outside to the gallows.

But after that murder trial, finding a jury became more difficult for Sheriff Howard. Life in raucous Virginia City mirrored very nearly life in the mines below. It was a beehive of activity 24 hours a day. This around-the-clock lifestyle also brought with it a preponderance of petty crime.

Daily there were fistfights and knifings, shootings and small isolated cases of suspected claim jumping, and each of these occurrences usually required a trial by jury. Trouble was, most of these episodes were generally viewed as everyday events by those hardened men on the Comstock, hardly worthy of "working up a sweat over." When faced with the choice of prospecting or sitting at the trial of somebody that "should not have even been arrested in the first place," the decision was clear. The hell with it. Suddenly, the good sheriff wasn't able to find jurors. The miners couldn't have cared less about routine court cases. The people of Nevada, it seemed, were adverse to being bull-whacked or badgered into doing anything.

Now such circumstances called for drastic measures. But the sheriff was quite up to the task. He decided that the one way to make sure that he could get people to show up for his trials was to create a little sensation of his own. And so he did. He resolved to create the most unusual, outrageous assortment of jurors that the city, indeed, the state had ever seen. His plan would go down in the annals of the legal profession as one of the most ingenious of the day.

When his next trial rolled around, he summoned only men who were cross-eyed, squinted-eyed or wall-eyed. He had to search the whole county to get them, but he got them—and for the first time in a long while, the courtroom was packed. Word spread about the most bizarre collection of characters "that could be seen anywhere," let alone in a courtroom.

For his next trial, Howard selected the fattest men in the territory. The jury box, said one William David, was "literally overflowing with flesh." So big were the men sequestered that the chairs had to be replaced with heavy benches. But the ruse worked. The community's concern was finally stirred. The crowds came and they loved it.

By now, Howard was on a roll and he knew it. People flocked to the courtroom not so much to witness a trial as to see what kind of a jury the sheriff would turn up with next.

They would not be disappointed. The next trial featured the county's thinnest men. In turn, it was followed by another, featuring the ugliest men. Lawyers were having such a hard time holding the attention of the courtroom, particularly of the jury itself, that they actually petitioned to have the sheriff's methods, indeed the sheriff himself if possible, banned from the courtroom. Howard, resigned to the fact that his time was running out, decided on one final fling.

He selected a jury that consisted of both the tallest and the shortest men in the area. One of the tallest, H.G. Blasdel, at 6 feet, 5 inches, would eventually go on to become a governor of the state. The shortest could barely reach over the rim of the jury box, and kept leaping up and waving wildly at the crowd. The sight of these men had its anticipated sideshow effect. The jury resembled the pipes on an organ more than an assembly of responsible citizenry.

The Howard trials would still go down the record books as some of the most popular and heavily attended of any in our history.

Those trials might not have been held at all, at least not without the efforts of a newly elected sheriff, a sheriff who decided that the best way to select a jury was to select them hilariously.

"RECALL NEVADA'S STATEHOOD!"

—Chicago Tribune headline—
After the passage of Nevada's gambling bill in 1931.

A WEAVER OF BASKETS
-33-

At one time, the Washo Indian tribe was the predominant force in Northern Nevada. Slowly their arch-rivals, the Paiutes, took command, driving the Washoes from their traditional home at the southern shore of Pyramid Lake, refusing them passage north of the Truckee River and forbidding them to own or even ride horses.

It was into this sad and ever-changing environment that she was born in 1834, before the first whites dared venture into the valley. During her lifetime, she would see the beginning of the end for her people, and the dawning of a new age. She became a chronicler of those troubled times, a historian of the first order. They called her Dat-So-La-Lee, and she was a weaver of baskets.

She was a giant woman, huge by any standards. Early historians claim that her name Dat-So-La-Lee means "Big Hips" but that story holds little weight today. In truth, it was often the custom of Washo and Paiutes alike to take the name of the family for which they worked. Her first employer was Dr. S.L. Lee. Whenever she was asked her name, she would try to answer "Dr. S.L. Lee." Dat-So-La-Lee was as close as she could manage.

Nevertheless, her baskets were stunning. Even today. their intricacy amazes artisans and scholars alike. They are true masterpieces of the ancient weavers' art. So incredible were those baskets that today they can be seen on display in the Peabody Collection at Yale University. Some of her other baskets can be seen at the Carnegie Institute in Pittsburgh and the Smithsonian in Washington, D.C. It is claimed that she was the only Indian weaver in the world that possessed a perfect knowledge of the value of perspective.

In this day of computerized design, it is unbelievable to behold the precision and care of Dat-So-La-Lee's baskets. In her lifetime, she created more than 3,000, many of which took years to complete. Some contain more than 100,000 individual stitches. On the average her works contains more than 30 stitches to the inch.

Never in her more than 80 years of weaving did she dye her materials. Her colors were always natural, light gold, white, and red, true colors prevalent in the Truckee Meadows. The task of collecting was monumental in itself.

She would create her own black thread from bracken roots dug during the spring. Red thread came the bark of red buds found only in the summer. In the fall, when the sap from the willows stopped running, she collected a substance from the area between the bark and the pith of branches, dried and cured it to create a thread that was almost pure white. So meticulous was she in selecting colors that some threads waited 20 years before being used.

It was after the materials had been painstakingly collected, however, that the real work began. With her teeth and fingernails, she would scrape the fibers and native plants until they were as thin as thread itself. Beginning with a tiny hole at the center of the base, Dat-So-La-Lee would add coil after coil. Lower rows, though seemingly of the same size to the naked eye, weighed more to provide stability. In each of the loops, she would carefully insert the threads of fiber, making certain that each thread was the exact consistency of the preceding one.

As the basket took shape, symbols were added using finer threads, the blending of which was so well done that the interior of the basket was every bit as smooth as the outside.

From her mother, she had been given the sacred right to record the history of her tribe, but tribal law also prohibited a weaver from duplicated any design previously made. By using certain symbols (similar to the European practice of suing a Coat of Arms or family crest) she was able to use variation to express a thought, a story, even a prayer.

It was an arduous task. When a basket was completed, in months or even years, her fingers would be raw and almost useless. Her eyes would be weakened into semi-blindness. As she always worked seated in the Indian fashion, she would walk stooped over for months at a time.

Nonetheless, her work went relatively unnoticed until a Carson City merchant, Able Cohn, became aware of her great talent.

Infatuated with her work, he built her a small cottage next to his home and for more than 35 years, she continued making baskets which would record the history of her people. Cohn even took her to the famous Arts and Crafts Exhibition in St. Louis in 1919, the only time she ventured from the Valley. She was heralded as a true American genius. In Nevada, her likeness (she refused to be photographed until she was near her death) began to appear on postcards sold on every corner.

But all the sudden attention mattered little to Dat-Sol-La-Lee. She would often respond to praise with a surly grunt; at times, with no reply at all. Many whites considered her rude and unfriendly.

As she neared death, a white physician attempted to attend to her. Instead, she requested the aid of 3 medicine men from her tribe. The ancient wisemen created a replica of a tribal medicine hut. They wrapped her in rabbit skins as custom demanded and she sat upright for 3 days until death came.

By the time she died, Dat-So-La-Lee had seen it all: the demise of her people, first at the hands of the Paiutes, then with the coming of the whites; she had seen the countryside overrun by the endless flocks of gold-seekers; she had seen the coming of the railroad, the telegraph, the telephone, and the automobile. Though she herself always refused to participate, she saw her people dress not in the manner of the native Washo, but in the manner of the northern Blackfeet, Crow and Sioux tribes. To her dismay, she saw them lead the Parade of Indians at the opening day of Reno's Rodeo. Yes, Dat-So-La-Lee had seen it all.

During her lifetime, her work commanded incredible prices, but through it all, she seemed almost unaware. Until her final illness, she had been working on a basket for which she had been offered $1,100, even in its unfinished state. On her death bed she asked that the basket not be sold, but rather that it be buried with her. Her request was granted.

SALOONS...
THEY JUST DON'T MAKE 'EM
LIKE THEY USED TO...
-34-

There was a time when the Western dominated the television screen. There was the Lone Ranger, Black Saddle, the Rifleman, Wanted: Dead or Alive, Bonanza, and of course, the venerable Gunsmoke. But did you ever notice? Most of the real action—the shootouts, the first fights, the steely eyed confrontations,—most of it took place in the saloon. Or, at the very least, in front of it.

Remember Gunsmoke? Old Matt Dillon spent more time in the Longbranch than in his own office. Now some of you old timers will probably say, "Well, wouldn't you? How else could he get to see Miss Kitty?" But at the risk of offending the fans of Amanda Blake, I have to tell you the truth. Women not withstanding, everything of real importance on the frontier took place in the saloon. That's why ol' Matt was hanging out there.

By necessity, the saloon was generally the first building constructed in any frontier town. Wrote one Nevada pioneer, "The first establishment was set up inside a tent. Soon there were 20 girls from we know not where. Then a pianoforte instrument was brought over the mountains on muleback at great trouble and expense. There were 12 such places going before the preacher even erected a church."

And no wonder. The local watering hole proved to be the ultimate meeting place. It usually served as a stage stop and hostelry combined. The preacher held forth on Sundays and the city fathers met there the rest of the week. Early mining claims were generally posted behind the plank and even the town's marshall usually set up shop inside, the theory being that since most of the excitement took place in the saloon anyway, why bother to look for other quarters?

Such a place was Virginia City's first saloon. Although it served its purpose admirably and made vast sums for its owner, it came about quite by accident.

It was March of the year 1860. John Moore, a drummer from San Francisco, had sunk his life savings, $1,600, into a wagonload of whiskey and headed for the gold fields of Hangtown, California (later Placerville) when a freak winter storm struck. He soon found the pass leading into the American River town blocked with snow. Realizing that he couldn't easily drink $1,600 worth of whiskey all by himself and running short of cash besides, Moore took a more northern Sierra route and luckily wound up in another boom town that was just beginning to make a name for itself, the fledgling Virginia City.

His decision would turn out to be profitable beyond his wildest dreams. When he arrived at the diggings, he learned that not only was whiskey in short supply, but lodging as well. John Moore immediately set out to remedy the situation.

He first erected a huge tent and divided it in two. On one side, he set up his saloon (really nothing more than two whiskey barrels connected by a couple of long planks) and on the other he rigged up some crude cots.

The money began pouring in the very first day. His whiskey business flourished and when his supply began to diminish, he simply added water accumulated from the melting snows. Immediately his overhead went down and his profits up. There were few complaints from the constabulary. The thirsty prospectors were happy to get any whiskey at all.

His "hotel" did even better. And no wonder, the prices he charged were nothing short of exorbitant—a dollar got you two blankets and a spot on the ground; for another 50 cents you received some padding and wood shavings from a nearby lumber mill. Still, it was the first saloon/hotel on the Comstock and as such, it earned a prominent place in the city's short history. Moore never bothered to try his hand prospecting. He was simply too busy making money from all those that did.

Soon he added a store of sorts, selling shovels for as much as $9.00, and flour and nails for $1.00 a pound! After a time, a real hotel, constructed of wood and stone, was erected on the site, and Moore, and wily drummer, went on to become a highly respected member of the community.

But such happenings were not unusual throughout Nevada. The man who provided the whiskey usually was one of the most

1 0 4

popular fellas in town. And not just because he sold frontier fortification, either. Quite simply, he usually made a heck of a lot more money that any of his customers. Many Nevada saloon keepers became mayors and more than a few actually went on to serve in the Senate.

Though saloons themselves were notorious as havens of violence and prostitution, even the usually fire-breathing clergy chose not to chastise saloon keepers too much. Said one member of the cloth back in 1869, "I have no quarrel with the local saloon. Should I find myself in need of a flock to which to preach, I have only to walk through its doors..."

There were few people around, good and bad alike, who would criticize such a business. In many saloons, there were ornately carved bars on display which had been transported by clipper ship around Cape Horn and then by wagon over the Sierra. Some measured more than 40 feet in length and for customers, it was standing room only. There was the lifesize painting of the beautiful woman, which was mandatory in every saloon, for the women themselves were actually few and far between. And there were also the obligatory mirrors, strategically located to make the establishment appear larger, an ingenious technique used in modern drinking halls, especially Nevada casinos, to this very day.

Sadly, the saloons of the frontier are gone now, living on only in the movies and in television reruns. Alas, as many an old timer will tell you, they just don't make saloons like they used to. They have gone the way of the corner grocery store, no longer places for meetings and companionship. I know I'll get letters in argument, of course, but they just don't make 'em like they used to when Matt Dillon and Miss Kitty were alive.

"Clemens had a great habit of making fun of the young fellows and the girls, and wrote ridiculous pieces about parties and other social events to which he was never invited. After a while he went over to Carson City and touched up the people over there and got everybody down on him. I thought he had faded from our midst forever, but the citizens of Carson drove him away.

"At any rate, he drifted back to Virginia City in a few weeks. He didn't have a friend, but the boys got together and said they would give a party and invite Clemens to it, and make him feel at home, and respectable and decent, and kindly, and generous, and loving, and considerate of the feelings of others. I could have warned them, but I didn't.

"Clemens went to that party and danced with the prettiest girls and monopolized them, and enjoyed himself, and made a good meal and then shoved over to the Enterprise office and wrote the whole thing up in an outrageous manner. He lambasted that party for all the English language would allow, and if any of the guests was unfortunate enough to be awkward or had big feet, or a wart on the nose, Clemens did not forget it.

"After that he drifted away, and I thought he had been hanged, or elected to Congress, or something like that, and I had forgotten him... I was confident he would come to no good end, but I have heard from him from time to time since then, and I understand that he has settled down and become respectable.

—United States Senator William Stewart—
Of his friend, the rambunctious Mark Twain

OLD NEWSPAPERS...
DON'T YA MISS 'EM?
-35-

I love gambling papers, don't you? Because they are fun to read. Turn the pages and there are pictures of people who have won the bout with Lady Luck, people who have tossed the dice and won, pulled the handle and come up winners. There are no stories on AIDS, no photos of Ollie North, no graphic descriptions of flag burnings or violence in China.

Newspapers have changed a great deal over the years. Gone are the days when those early tabloids made up the news when things were slow or lambasted the politicos in no uncertain terms. I miss the old papers, I really do. That's why when somebody loans me one of them, I'm ecstatic, like a kid with a new toy.

Donna Zenz of Sparks loaned me her faded edition of the *Silver State*, published up in Winnemucca on July 3, 1894. It's just filled with what I like to call "the good stuff," ads, articles and little bits wisdom that we have regretfully lost in our more modern publications. Today, newspaper humor is generally confined to one page of comics and perhaps (depending on your point of view) to columns like Dear Abby. I, for one, say they just don't make newspapers like they used to.

For example, there in the upper left hand corner of the *Silver State* (looking for all the world like an editorial) is an advertisement entitled "Knowledge." Underneath, a woodcut shows a buxom and bustled young lady demurely holding a long-stemmed glass to her lips. The copy reads, "Knowledge brings comfort and improvement and tends to personal enjoyment when rightly used. The many who live better than others and enjoy life more, with less expenditure, by more promptly adapting the world's best products to the needs of the physical being, will attest to the value of health and the pure liquid laxative principles embraced in the remedy Syrup of Figs."

Syrup of figs? Yep.

"Its excellence is due to its presenting in the form most acceptable and pleasant to the taste, effectively cleansing the system, dispelling colds, headaches and fevers and permanently curing constipation. It has met with the approval of the medical profession because it acts on the kidney, liver and bowels without weakening them and it is perfectly free from every objectionable substance."

The article goes on to explain that Syrup of Figs can be obtained for the measly sum of 50 cents, and that the buyer should beware of any imitations.

Mrs. Winslow's Soothing Syrup was another one. "Used by millions of mothers while their babies are teething!

"If disturbed at night and broken of your rest by a sick child suffering and crying with pain, send at once and get a bottle. It cures diarrhea, regulates the stomach and the bowels, cures wind colic, and gives tone and energy to the whole system." It was sold by all druggists "throughout the world," for "one low price of just 25 cents."

Sarsaparilla seems to have a popular item. The *State's* second page boasts not one, but three separate ads for the stuff, each offering to cure an entirely different ailment.

One, Ayer's Sarsaparilla ("Has Cured Others Will Cure You!"), cured skin of "Pimples, Boils, Blotches and the Rash."

Another promised faithfully that if suffering a bout with Typhoid, "A Marvelous Cure" would help, "after all else failed." The ad went on to describe how Mrs. Phoebe Hall of Galva, Kansas was "At Death's door before taking Hood's Sarsaparilla." Must have been powerful stuff.

The third ad, entitled "The Spring Medicine," read, "All worn down from the weakening effects of warm weather? You need a good tonic and blood purifier. Do not put off taking Sarsaparilla. Numerous little ailments, if neglected, will soon break up the system. This product will expel disease and give you strength and appetite." Gee, I wonder what it would do for my cholesterol count?

Not to be outdone, some of the claims even carried a money-back guarantee. There was this tiny ad buried deep in the body of the paper: "We offer One Hundred Dollars reward for any case of Catarrh that cannot be cured by Hall's Catarrh Cure. We, the undersigned, have known the manufacturer, F.J. Cheney, for the last 15 years and he is perfectly able to carry out all business obligations made by his firm. Hall's Catarrh Cure is taken directly upon the blood and mucous surfaces of the system. There is no finer cure available!"

Yep, it was almost as much fun reading the ads as it was reading the articles. An advertisement for the Eagle Drug Store in Winnemucca promised "All goods sold at San Francisco prices," and an ad for the Palace, a small drinking establishment, which boasted not only the "finest brands of wines, liquors and cigars," but more importantly, a "Free Lunch Counter!" The Reception Restaurant featured fresh baked bread at 10 cents a loaf and even an oyster grotto, though how they managed to get oysters out in the middle of the desert is a mystery.

How about this one: "When you feel cross as a cat,' a dose of Ayer's Pills will make you as good natured as a kitten. Try them for biliousness! Works every time!"

Yessiree, I just love these old newspapers. No one really thought to question much of what was printed, and the majority of what was written was simply taken as gospel. Even today, the old newspapers of Nevada still provide a wondrous and often humorous glimpse into the past, a glimpse of days done by, uncomplicated times that unfortunately, we will never see again.

Oh well, this is 1989, and we're stuck with it . So now back to the news and more stories about plague and pestilence, pollution and such...

EAT YOUR HEART OUT, DON KING!
-36-

Everybody knows Don King. He's the promoter's promoter, the frizzy-haired entrepreneur who skyrocketed Mohammed Ali to worldwide fame and who has been seen in the corners of the most famous fighters on the planet ever since.

But King has nothing on one of the very first promoter-managers, an obscure but affable fellow by the name of Billy Nolan. Nolan's uncanny ability to secure the edge for his fighter first came to light in the mining camp of Goldfield.

Tex Rickard, a saloon owner who would go on to fame and fortune as the man who created the largest gate in fight history with his Dempsey-Tunney match years later, had dreamed up the idea of holding a championship fight in Goldfield. It seems that the tiny but raucous city, once one of the richest boomtowns in the west, had fallen on hard times. As the output from the silver mines declined and fickle prospectors and investors headed for greener pastures, so did Rickard's profits. He decided a prize fight would be just the solution.

Many thought Rickard mad. After all, Goldfield, Nevada wasn't exactly New York, Chicago, Denver or San Francisco—there were less than 3,000 residents and they were tentative residents at best. Just the same, Rickard was convinced that a fight would be the saving grace of Goldfield, and he set out to secure two of the best: Battling Nelson, known affectionately as "the gentle Dane," and the lightweight Champion Joe Gans.

Enter Billy Nolan, wily manager of the Dane. When first approached by Rickard, who offered the then-unheard of purse of $15,000 for the fight, Nolan balked. In later years, some said that he declined the offer thinking that such an exorbitant fee was merely a practical joke. But it didn't matter, for Nolan just doubled the price—to $30,000. Rickard accepted and the contest was on.

Rickard was, in his own right, a promoter himself. As soon as the purse had been agreed upon, he promptly arranged for the entire amount to be displayed in the window of his main street business, a saloon and gambling hall called the Northern, which boasted "the longest bar in the west," a 50-foot plank served by more than a dozen mixologists. True to form, when Nolan first stopped by to view the hoard of coins, he requested that the fight contract be amended. For that amount of money, said Nolan, the bout should be "winner take all." Eventually he settled for two thirds of the prize money. But it would not be the last of his many attempts to gain the upper hand for his fighter.

His next chance came almost immediately. Each of the fighters had set up their training camps on the outskirts of town. The easy-going Gans threw his quarters open to the public. Miners, gandy dancers and reporters alike were welcome to watch the champion train each morning, and even treated to ringside seats at impromptu sparring matches.

But things were not so friendly across town. Nolan not only roped off the entire grounds, but he threw a big canvas wall around the training ring, forbidding even the press entry, unless they paid a "small" fee of $1. This move infuriated the town of Goldfield and many immediately placed their money on the black champion, although prejudice was rampant at the time.

The response was just what the wily Nolan had anticipated. Not only was he able to pull down an incredible $1,000 a day in additional profits, but he had managed to increase the odds against his fighter. He quickly poured some of his training receipts back into the betting pool. The irate newspaper stories soon became much easier to bear.

Learning that the aging opponent had a weight problem and was planning on eating a hearty meal shortly before the fight, at the last minute, Nolan insisted that the weigh-in be held, not on the morning of the fight, but at ringside. Nevertheless, the amiable Gans agreed.

Nolan increased his demands further still. He would refuse to let Nelson enter the ring, he said, unless both fighters were weighed in their trunks and shoes, a ploy that would obviously add several pounds. Gans literally starved himself for the last 36 hours before the contest and though considerably weakened, stepped on the scales at precisely the required weight, 133 pounds.

Gans was the sleeker and more experienced of the two. The Dane was cumbersome, often lumbering around the ring, wildly flailing his arms in an attempt to land a damaging blow. Throughout the devastating 42 rounds, before more than 7,000 screaming fight fans, Nelson landed blows that fell well below their mark. The referee, George Siler, warned Nelson continuously about low punches.

The fight ended when Nelson landed yet another kidney punch and Gans collapsed in agonizing pain. Siler stopped the fight and awarded the win to Gans.

Nolan was not ready to concede, however. He leapt into the ring, arguing that Rickard's event had been a fraud from the beginning. He demanded that Gans forfeit his winnings.

When Rickard refused, Nolan hired an attorney and instigated legal proceedings. He went so far as to purchase films of the fight (the first championship battle ever recorded by the infant industry) and had stills made. He had the photos blown up life-size and placed strategically throughout the town. The picture seemed to indicate that referee Siler had been at Gans' back and could not possibly have seen "any low blow." Now many other spectators were saying that "all bets were off." Some demanded their money back.

In the end, however, it was a Chicago newspaper that laid to rest the decision once and for all. The following week, a newspaper arrived from the windy city and there, splattered across the front page, was a photo showing the final moment of the fight. Sure enough, there, for all to see, was Nelson delivering the low blow. The decision was upheld.

The Champion Gans would soon retire, followed closely by Nelson, who, despite the efforts of Billy Nolan, would never again enjoy the limelight. But two of the four who had participated in the incredible "$30,000 Battle of the Century" would remain friends for many years. Promoter Rickard, who would soon become world-famous himself, often shared ringside seats with the ex-fighter, and frequently had the now-punch-drunk Nelson as a guest in his home.

Of the four men, only Rickard would go on to the notoriety that Don King today enjoys. He would continue to promote championship bouts until his dying day, when his body lay in state in a solid bronze coffin in the center of the ring at his beloved

111

Madison Square Garden.

I can't help but think that even Don King would have been proud of all of them...

"[The State Capitol] lies about 30 miles south of Reno, in circular Eagle Valley. It is a beautiful, homelike community adorned with flowers and tree-lined streets. The redoubtable Kit Carson had been there, and in the neighboring Carson Valley in the early '30s; settlers came about 20 years afterward, but not until 1858 was the city laid out. The founder was Abe Curry, picturesque pioneer.

"At first the settlement had a troubled existence, with a swarm of desperadoes to contend against, but after Sam Brown [notorious badman] fell before the shotgun of Harry Van Sickle and after the Vigilance Committee staged a hanging or two, the peaceable element gained ascendancy.

"During the meeting of the legislature, the capitol was over-run with Comstock journalists and politicians. At all times, the place was a hotbed of electioneering activity. Caucuses, county conventions, ratification meetings and jollification meetings kept the political pot boiling...

—Editor Wells Drury—
Remembering early Carson City

PAT McCARRAN...
THE VIOLENT ROAD TO THE
UNITED STATES SENATE
-37-

There have been a lot of stories about Nevada in the news lately. We're high on the list of places where the feds would like to hide some nuclear waste (we're against it!) and low on the list of places where the new secret military installation could be built (we're for it!).

Still, presidents don't stop here often. You don't see a lot of interviews with our delegates at political conventions. As a result, most people think that Nevada doesn't have much clout in our nation's capitol. Nothing could be further from the truth for a state with so much land and so little population.

It began, of course, with President Lincoln. There he was, a president besieged with doubt over a bloody civil war and faced with slim chances for reelection. In desperation, Lincoln looked about for another state which could swing the balance of power and bring an end to slavery and to war. His scheme was successful. Nevada was grated statehood, Lincoln won another term, and for the first time, folks out here became respectable in the eyes of powerful eastern politicians.

That link continues right up to the present day when, before his retirement, Senator Paul Laxalt was about as close to President Reagan as a fella can get. Along the way, there was Howard Cannon who, it was said, "could get more done in a back room than most senators could accomplish in endless days on the floor."

But of all the politicians who have represented Nevadans on the banks of the Potomac, perhaps none was more influential than Senator Pat McCarran, who began his career on the dusty streets of Tonopah and went on to the hallowed halls of Congress with "a glib tongue, a ready wit, and tenacity born of the frontier."

Those folks who are new to the Silver State still come across his illustrious name on a daily basis. There are boulevards and back streets in Reno which bear his name, and a great airport facility in Las Vegas. Few newcomers realize, however, that unlike most politicians today, McCarran started small, as a country lawyer in the lawlessness of a raucous boomtown just after the turn of the century.

"Popular Sheriff Killed," screamed the headline of the *Tonopah Bonanza* back in April of 1906. "Tom Logan murdered in cold blood by a gambler!"

It was true, of course. Sheriff Tom Logan, one of the most popular lawmen in the outstate, had been shot by Walt Barieau, a professional card player who frequented the gambling halls of Manhattan. Even in 1906, there was talk of forming a lynch mob and giving justice a helping hand.

Although there was little doubt that he had fired the fatal shots, Barieau pleaded innocent and threw himself at the mercy of the court. He admitted that he "gambled from time to time," but claimed that he was "a family man, poor in the ways of the legal system." Declaring himself a pauper, he asked the court to appoint an attorney for his defense.

Enter Pat McCarran.

McCarran had been admitted to the bar less than a year before, and had yet to try an important case. In later years he would admit, "I had never believed that a man could feel such fear...that his legs would tremble beneath him. I finally realized what it was like to be totally possessed by fear, embarrassment and consternation!"

McCarran cautiously agreed to accept the case. While the *Bonanza* continued to rant and rave about the "grave injustice" that had been done, McCarran stalled for time. When several stays were granted, he took advantage of that time to check into the background of the two men.

Like a modern-day Matlock, he began to uncover a few interesting facts. It seemed that both the defendant and the popular sheriff had been involved with the same girl, a woman of questionable virtue. The sheriff, as well as Barieau, had visited her on many occasions and saloon conversation had it that both were vying for her somewhat substantial favors.

In the courtroom, McCarran painted an insidious portrait of betrayal and deceit. The sheriff, he claimed, was a womanizer, a man who would do anything to keep the woman that he loved. Barieau, on the other hand, was "a faithful family man," the sole provider for a wife and 8 children who would "die in poverty" without the support of their 'oving father.

So gripping was his performance, that soon the *Tonopah Bonanza* was singing quite a different tune. Front page stories sung the praises of the budding lawyer who "brought tears to the eyes of the entire courtroom." Barieau was no longer a "cold-blooded killer," but an honest citizen forced to react to the "cruelty" of the law.

After 17 hours of deliberation, Barieau was acquitted. McCarran had successfully convinced the press, the townsfolk, and most importantly, the jury, of Barieau's innocence. Justice had been served. McCarran would parlay that success into the seat of District Attorney for Nye County.

The rest, as they say, is history. Pat McCarran, country lawyer, eventually leapfrogged into the United States Senate, a position of power that he, as well as Nevada, would enjoy for many years.

Scholars have attributed his popularity to the fact that the constituents of Nevada came first for the senator, before the interests of Pat McCarran himself, before even the interests of the country.

And perhaps it was true. When mobster Bugsy Seigal was attempting to open the Flamingo Hotel, the first major hotel in the city of Las Vegas, along came Pat McCarran to the rescue. He knew full well that Bugs had been a hit man for the Mob, and that most of his financing was coming from an east coast distiller which served as a front for organized crime. Nevertheless, McCarran was highly sensitive to Nevada's desire to bring more business into Las Vegas, and aware that most Nevadans didn't care where the money was coming from.

Seigal was having trouble getting building supplies before McCarran stepped in. There was a war on, and materials were in short supply. After a couple of well-placed phone calls, soon the ban was lifted, allowing the Flamingo to rise from the desert floor.

How did he do it? He managed to convince the federal government that "thousands of people in southern Nevada" were "aiding the war effort," and desperately needed "satisfactory living quarters in order to finish their work."

Senator Pat McCarran had come a long, long way from the bustling town of Tonopah. And Nevada has never been quite the same since.

NEVADA'S GUARD, BATTLE BORN!
-38-

Nineteen hundred and eighty-seven: that was the year of our Constitution. That year we celebrated 200 years of law in the land that most world countries refer to as the States that are United.

Most of the hoopla, of course, centered around the men in Philadelphia. There they were in the sweltering heat, trying to pound out a statement though would, hopefully, forever govern the 13 colonies. It was an almost impossible task, and as you know if you've followed a few of those features that newspapers, radio and television blitzed you with, hardly anyone was in agreement.

A basic argument centered around a standing army, a force of men who could be counted upon to defend the fledgling America. There was little doubt that some type of an army was needed. After all, ol' George and company had done well, hadn't they? Such as it was, the Continental Army had whipped the greatest military power on earth. They had beaten the British back across the ocean. America was free of tyranny.

But underlying the meeting in Philadelphia was that nagging fear. The great monarchs of Europe had used their armies for centuries to enslave the people, to impose taxes, to bend entire cities to their will. With a standing army in America, could not the same thing happen here?

In the end, of course, the majority opted for an army, such as it was. Many states decided to maintain separate armies of their own, similar to the groups of volunteers that had answered the call when the British first landed. Call them minutemen, rangers, militia, they were volunteers all. They were the beginning of what we have come to call our National Guard.

Perhaps nowhere in America has the Guard played a more pivotal role than right here in the Silver State, where a ragtag group of volunteers first brought order to an infant territory.

It was 1860 when the word came down. Nevada's Paiutes were restless. For almost a decade, they had watched helplessly as more and more settlers had progressed across Nevada. At first they had tried to be friendly to the whites. In fact, old Chief Truckee had guided the famous John Fremont and his scout Kit Carson through the area on their original mapping expedition.

But the flow of humanity grew. By 1848, it is estimated that 22,000 settlers had crossed the territory en route to Oregon and California. By the following year, when word of the discovery of gold in California had reached the eastern seaboard, that number had more than doubled, to 45,000. By 1852, more than 52,000 settlers were on their way to the Promised Land. In the process, they tore up the fragile desert home of the Paiutes, who tried their very best to remain friendly.

It took the discovery of a soft bluish substance called silver to bring an end to the life the Indians of Nevada had known. Suddenly, in 1859, James Finney and his partners uncovered what would become the richest ore strike on earth. Now, instead of passing through on the way to someplace else, thousands of people were heading **"to"** Nevada.

It happened at tiny Williams Station. A band of Indians suddenly swooped down on the settlement, killing the stationmaster and a hired hand. When news of the "massacre" (if, indeed, that was what it was) reached the boomtown of Virginia City, the word went out to the surrounding camps. Soon a group of men under the command of Major Ormsby left Carson City in hot pursuit.

At a point along the Truckee River (which by now bore the name of the friendly Paiute), some 3 miles from Pyramid Lake, the volunteers came upon a band of Indians and attacked. The Indians withdrew and the whites, flushed with a quick victory, followed— right into an ambush. Of the original group of 105 volunteers, only 29 survived.

Anton Kauffman was only 16 at the time, still wet behind the ears. But he survived the attack and would later write of his commanding officer, "The bravest thing I ever saw was Captain Watkins, wounded and leaning on a crutch blazing away at the Indians."

But that defeat only served to strengthen the resolve of the men along the frontier. A group of men who called themselves the Washoe Regiment was hastily organized. Comprised mainly of farmers, prospectors, ranchers and miners (very few of which were familiar with firearms), they formed 8 companies of infantry and 6 of cavalry. On May 24th, they left Virginia City on a forced march.

Below Dayton, a scout was sent out who never returned. Fearlessly, the men continued onward. The number of volunteers was by then swelling to more than 700.

The accounts of what happened next are now blurred by time. But what would become known as the Battle of Pyramid Lake, the only real major Indian fight in Nevada's history, was short and decisive. The Indians, heavily outnumbered, were swiftly defeated. Once more there was peace in the Territory.

It was the beginning of a tradition, a tradition that has lasted until the present day. It was the birth of Nevada's own National Guard. There would be difficult times ahead, to be sure. In 1883, the Guard Adjutant wrote to Governor J.W. Adams, "The fame of the National Guard of Nevada has the same sterling ring among military organizations as our gold and silver production has among the civilized nations that look to Nevada for its production." The officer, Charles Laughton, was appealing not for pay for his troops, but for funds to provide arms and ammunition. The usual ration was 100 rounds per man, and that was to last an entire year. Not a single bullet could be wasted.

Between the years 1906 and 1928, Nevada was the only state in the Union not to have a National Guard at all, due to a lack of funding from an already overextended legislature. Regardless, the state provided more than 900 percent of its allotted quota of men at the outbreak of the First World War.

What began that day along the banks of the Truckee River back in the year 1860 were the roots of the Nevada National Guard. No wonder the official motto of the State whose name it bears is "Battle Born."

"Jim Townsend was a unique specimen, by all odds the most original writer and versatile liar that the west coast, or any other coast, ever produced. He began his journalistic career in Mono County, California and wound up in Carson City, where so many newspapers lie buried. He kept the entire west laughing with quaint sayings which he set up...as they came into his mind.

"To read his paper you would think that it was published in a city of ten thousand inhabitants. He had a mayor and a city council, whose proceedings he reported once a week, although they never existed, and enlivened his columns with killings, law suits, murder trials and railroad accidents, and a thousand incidents of daily life in a humming growing town —every last one of which he coined out of his own active brain."

—Editor Wells Drury—
Writing about the common practice of "making up" the news.

MARRIED AT 14...
NEVADA'S FIRST WEDDING
-39-

Women They were few and far between in early Nevada, especially near the diggings. In the early days of Gold hill, the arrival of a member of the fair sex was such an occasion that it brought miners from miles around. A glimpse of a woman, any woman, regardless of beauty or even age, would be the topic of conversation for literally months on end.

There were always women there, of course. Quick on the heels of the first wooden buildings usually came the cribs, the small untidy clapboard hostelries which were hastily erected for the ladies of the evening. It was not uncommon for the men to utilize the services of a marriage broker, someone who could arrange a marriage by mail. The family men would send for wives and children only when they had come across a find large enough to merit staying in one place, an uncommon occurrence in the daily life of most itinerant prospectors.

During Nevada's infancy, towns sprung up almost overnight and then, just as suddenly, they disappeared again. One moment a grouping of several hundred tents would be the center of frenzied activity as the miners scrambled over the hillsides with reckless abandon. The next moment, those same tents would be gone. Completely. Without a trace. They would just vanish. Even at their best, those tents hardly provided adequate living conditions for anyone, let alone women.

In the summer of 1853, a man by the name of Powell arrived in Gold Canyon. Unlike most of the miners in the region, Powell had two small children in tow, one, a girl barely 14. His wife had recently passed away and Powell, unwilling to give up his dream of striking it rich in the Nevada range, simply brought the youngsters along. Little did he know that his daughter would be the first woman to be married in the Silver State. In addition, she would

119

also hold the rather dubious distinction of being the first woman in Nevada to be granted a divorce.

Life at the diggings during that first year would prove incredibly difficult for the family. That initial winter would bury the mountain in snow drifts up to 8 feet deep, while winds whipped along the divide at more than 60 miles an hour. Wisely forsaking the tent city that had emerged on the edge of the canyon, Powell was able to find lodging for his son and daughter in a new boarding house in Gold Hill. Admonishing them to be good and to "stay clear of confidence men," he packed up his tools and headed off into 6 Mile Canyon.

But word spread rapidly. There was a woman at the boarding house, a "real" woman. There was hardly a mention of the fact that she was barely into her teens. It didn't matter. Men of all ages, colors and creeds converged on the building on the false pretense of inquiring about a room. Some even offered to pay astronomical amounts for nothing more than a small cot down in the stone basement.

Among them was a Missouri bachelor named Benjamin Cole.

Like Powell himself, Cole had followed the legend of California riches west. Finding most of the good claims already played out, he soon retraced his steps back over the Sierra and into the Utah Territory. It didn't take him long to learn about the Powell girl. He began an ardent courtship and within a matter of days after her father had departed, Cole had convinced the youngster that she should marry him.

The camp was divided equally in their sentiments. Some of the miners sided with the new man Cole. After all, the lack of women in the Territory and the incredible loneliness of the barren mountainside was something with which each of them could easily identify.

But there were others who sympathized with the absent father. Although many girls of the period, especially those with southern roots, were normally married early in their teens, many of the men had children of their own and worried for the girl's safety.

Just the same, Cole's zealous wooing paid off. He and the Powell girl were married in a small ceremony in her boarding house. The following day, newlywed Benjamin Cole, in much the same manner as the girl's father, left his bride of 24 hours in the very same boarding house and took off in search of the elusive El

Dorado.

Within a week, Powell returned to Gold Hill. He was furious when learned that far from "staying clear of confidence men," his only daughter had actually married one. Brandishing a shotgun, he went off in search of the Missourian, only to learn that he had left the diggings. Without delay, Powell bustled up his two children and headed for what he thought would the safety of California.

But they would not be safe for long. Cole soon appeared at the diggings, and learning that his new wife had suddenly left him, he marshalled a group of his friends and they set off in rapid pursuit, riding through both day and night in a feverish attempt to overtake the fleeing father.

The impromptu posse caught up with the Powell family just as they were preparing the cross the Sierra. There were heated words on both sides. Powell claimed that his daughter was too young to marry, while Cole held fast to his conviction that the two were in love and as such, should be allowed the usual pleasures of wedded bliss.

In the end, faced with the tears of the two children and the old but deadly shotgun held menacingly by the father, Benjamin Cole reluctantly agreed to give up his young bride. Powell and the children were allowed to continue on into California under the condition that they would never again set foot in Nevada. Cole returned to Gold Canyon and the diggings emptyhanded.

Nevada's first marriage was short-lived. The following month, Benjamin Cole requested a divorce and it was granted. The union had lasted only a matter of days, but it would go down in the history books of the budding Nevada territory as not only the first marriage ever recorded, but the shortest...

THE STAGE DRIVER...
AN INCREDIBLE BREED
-40-

The stage coach driver. He was quite a fella. A legend.

Today it is difficult to imagine that there was a time in the history of America when the stagecoach was the only means by which to get from Point A to Point B. During the trip, which in some cases covered more than 60 miles, it was not unusual for the coach to ford rivers up to 8 feet deep, traverse mountain passes so rugged that boulders had to be muscled out of the way and tree branches brushed aside. A lucky day for a passenger was, when faced with a steep grade, he was forced to walk. On an unlucky day, he had to get out and push, often in knee-deep mud or snow.

Know anybody who drives a truck? One of those 18-wheelers? My father-in-law drives one and I'm still amazed when I see him back a 40 foot rig into a loading dock with the gentle touch of a hospital surgeon. Back 100 years ago, any stagecoach driver worth his salt could do much the same thing, and he could do it with eight restless horses in front of him. Those stage coach drivers were incredible men.

Their names still spring from the pages of history books—men like Hank Monk, Ben Dasher and Baldy Green. They carried passengers, the mail and the wealth from the mines. But most importantly, they carried the news. In many isolated Nevada towns, they were the only connection with the outside world, and folks left homes and businesses when word flashed along the main street, "Coach comin' in!"

The work was perilous, the pay poor. Heavy leather reins choked the fingers of each hand and threatened to pull the arms from their sockets. Eyes already strained by high winds, pelting rain and billowing dust were constantly searching for the slightest obstruction in the road ahead, then sweeping the passing terrain for any sign of marauding Indians or highwaymen. Wind, landslides, floods—they were part of the daily fare. But somehow, hardship not withstanding, they usually got through.

Long before television and movies, the stage coach driver were immortalized by early papers and popular dime novels. Nevada's legendary Hank Monk was featured in print by newspaperman Horace Greeley. While on his first trip west, Greeley was given what he called "the ride of my life," en route to Hangtown with Monk at the reins. The journey so terrified the Easterner that he refused to ride in another coach for months afterward. Readers, as well as Hank Monk, loved it.

In 1877, there were more than 30 stage line operating out of bustling Virginia City, each employing a score of drivers and a minimum of 3 coaches. The winding, twisting road from the valley floor up the treacherous Geiger Grade became famous as one of the most difficult in the entire west, a roadway so narrow that in many places, passengers leaning out the window could see no road at all, just a drop of more than 200 feet.

Sometimes, the journey was so arduous that it was necessary for the passengers themselves to lend a hand. On one occasion, a stage descending from Virginia City struck a boulder and catapulted the driver completely off the coach. The team, hearing the stricken cries of the passengers, bolted down the mountain side at breakneck speed. Ned Boyle, superintendent of the Alta Mine, was aboard, and without hesitation, he leaned out the window and shot one of the lead horses, saving the lives of everyone on board. The other animals jerked to a stop just inches from the edge of a yawning chasm. It is interesting to note that the event would make history in another way—Ned Boyle's son Emmet would eventually go on to become a governor of the state of Nevada.

One of the most renowned drivers of the Virginia City-Carson run was Baldy Green, who made the trip twice daily. As stage drivers go, he was an affable fellow, liked by all who knew him for his spellbinding tall tales of his own colorful exploits. But Baldy had one small problem: he was held up a great deal, so much that even the robbers developed a liking for him.

So numerous were the holdups that Baldy was involved in that the raucous actually composed a song about Baldy Green. At a premier performance held at Piper's Opera House, Baldy, the guest of honor, was greeted by a barber shop quartet. Comstock reporter Alf Doten recalled the lyrics:

I'll tell you all a story
And I'll tell it in a song,
I hope that it will please you
For it won't detain you long.
Tis about one of the old boys,
So gallus and so fine,
Who used to carry mails
On the Pioneer Line.

He was the greatest favor-ite
That ever yet was seen
He was known about Virginia
By the name of Baldy Green.
Oh, he swung a whip so gracefully,
He was bound to shine,
For he was a high toned driver
On the Pioneer Line.

Now as he was driving out one night
As lively as a coon,
He saw 3 men jump in the road
By the pale light of the moon.
Two sprung for the leaders
While one his shotgun cocks,
Saying, 'Baldy, we hate to trouble you
But pass us out the box.'

When Baldy heard them say these words,
He opened wide his eyes.
He didn't know what in the world to do
for it took him by surprise.
Then he reacted into the boot saying,
'Take it boys, with pleasure,'
So out into the middle of the night
went Wells and Fargo's treasure.

Now when they got the treasure box,
they seemed quite satisfied,
For the men who held the leader
Now politely stepped aside.

Saying 'Baldy, we got what we want,
So drive along your team.'
And he made the quickest time to Silver City
Ever seen!

Don't say 'Greenbacks' to Baldy now.
It makes him feel so sore.
He'd traveled the road many a time
and was never stopped before.
Oh, the chances they were 3 to 1
And shotguns were the game.
If you'd a been in Baldy's place,
You'd a' shelled her out the same!

Nevada's kings of the road—stage coach drivers. They fought the elements, the bandits, the rugged terrain, not to mention the clock, to bring civilization to the region. For a time, they formed the only tenacious link between Nevada's boomtowns, a sprawling network that would eventually become unified as a state.

They are gone now, of course, replaced by modern day "kings" who, with 350 horses, computers, and a capacity of more than 70,000 pounds, can cruise effortlessly along our super highways at 80 plus. For a time, however, the men at the rein were the stuff of which legends are made. Sadly, we will not see their like again...

"Nevadans do not worry over abuses as much as an Easterner, simply because he is used to minding his own business. East of the Missouri no one minds his own business, but west of the river people really do mind it.

"I do not mean to hold up the sovereign state of Nevada as an example of legal purism. Nor is it an especially law-abiding state. It is wild country, most of it, pretty well unredeemed to civilization. Perhaps the only laws that they respect are laws that give, not curtail freedom. They more or less ride steeplechases over the rest I fear...

—Author Katherine Geroald—
1925

THE DEATH OF
MEAN SAM BROWN
-41-

Sam Brown was a mean one, alright. Of all the desperados on the Comstock—a group that included such colorful characters as Six-Fingered Pete, Pock-Marked Jake and El Dorado Johnny—Sam Brown was the baddest of them all.

While most legends of the outlaws of the old west were far more fiction than fact, Sam Brown was the one true exception. Feared by all for his lightning temper, he openly cruised the saloons of Virginia City, his two guns constantly at the ready. He was known to head a band of men who had been involved in several holdups on Geiger Grade and rumor had it that Brown himself had more than a score of killings to his credit.

Even law officers gave Sam Brown a conveniently wide berth. Like something from the pages of a dime novel, when Sam Brown appeared, the bravest of men chose to walk on the other side of the street. To such veteran reporters as Dan DeQuille and Mark Twain, he was known simply as "The Chief."

The story began in Nevada's first townsite, the tiny settlement of Genoa. One of Brown's gang of cutthroats had been taken into custody for a killing that had taken place near the diggings. By the time the outlaw was brought before Judge Cradlebaugh in a Genoa courtroom, the public was up in arms. Newspapers were openly calling for a quick conviction and an even swifter public hanging. The power and reputation of the prosecutor, William Stewart, a powerful attorney who was already being considered as a sure bet for the United States Congress, added to the excitement.

But Sam Brown wasn't about to take the trial of one his gang lightly. He bragged openly to friends in Virginia City that he would soon appear in that Genoa courtroom and set his companion free, even if he had to do it over the dead body of William Stewart. He boasted that he would present his own account of the shooting and that no one would dare dispute him. It was only a matter of days before Sam Brown made good his threat.

When he walked into the courtroom, however, he found Stewart to be a more than formidable opponent. As Brown approached the bench, the strapping Stewart pulled two derringers from the pockets of his coat. Taking the gunman completely by surprise, he barked, "Now Mr. Brown, you have bragged that you would come down here and swear this defendant free and make this court accept your testimony. I am here to tell you," growled Stewart menacingly, "that if you attempt any of your gunplay or give any false testimony, I will blow your fool brains out!"

Faced with two cocked pistols, Brown quickly and wisely backed down. He told the court that he had not even considered attempting to free his comrade, that he had actually come to town to obtain the services of Stewart himself. As a hush fell over the courtroom, Brown reached into his pocket and took out a roll of bills. Offering $500 to Stewart, he asked the attorney to represent him in a pending California assault case. Nonplused, Stewart calmly pocketed the money. Brown then asked that court be adjourned and offered to stand everyone to a round of drinks in a nearby saloon. It appeared that the matter had been laid to rest.

It was not for long. As the liquor continued to flow, Brown was heard remarking to a friend that it was his thirtieth birthday, that his honor had been sullied and that he "had to have a man for supper." By then thoroughly liquored up, he mounted his horse and rode off toward Virginia City.

It was nightfall when Brown reined in at the courtyard of a wayside inn owned by one Henry Van Sickle. Although accounts of what took place vary slightly—including one written by Van Sickle himself and another penned by lawyer Stewart—most agree that the following conversation took place.

"Shall I put up your horse, Mr. Brown?" inquired the host.

"Hello, Van," came a cheery reply. "How are you feeling?"

Responded Van Sickle, "Tip top."

Then suddenly, Sam Brown pulled a gun and opened fire on the unarmed innkeeper, saying "You look like you're feeling too damn good. I'll take a shot at you for luck!"

But the luck was Van Sickle's. In the quickly falling darkness, the bullets missed, and the terrified Van Sickle ran to the safety of the inn.

With his smoking pistol still in hand, Brown followed. Crazed with liquor and bent on vengeance, the outlaw burst through the door of the popular rest stop. Guests who were sitting down to eat scattered in all directions. But the killer was unwilling to confront Van Sickle in front of so many witnesses, and abruptly retreated. In a white rage, he mounted his horse and rode off again.

But unbeknownst to the fleeing outlaw, Van Sickle had decided to take matters into his own hands. Knowing Brown's fearsome reputation and afraid he would return to finish the job, Van Sickle armed himself with a shotgun. Rather than waiting meekly at the inn, he mounted a horse and rode off in pursuit.

About a mile up the road, he overtook Brown, and leveling the shotgun, he unloaded with both barrels, knocking the badman from the saddle. Somehow, the wounded outlaw managed to mount again, but this time Van Sickle caught up with him more easily. Crying out,"I've finally got you. Now I kills you!" the innkeeper opened up a second and final time. The body of Sam Brown was found the next morning by the roadside. It bore the effects of the deadly shotgun blasts. For good measure, the body had also been peppered with more than a dozen bullets.

The reign of terror of one of the most feared badmen on the Comstock had come to an end. An obviously relieved coroner's jury noted sagely that Brown "had come to his death from a just dispensation of an all-wise Providence." Wrote the public-spirited foreman, "It served him right."

It was over. Sam Brown, without a doubt the meanest man in the young territory of Nevada, was buried without ceremony.

THE GHOST DANCE
OF WOVOKA
-42-

It was in 1889 when the Great Spirit appeared to Jack Wilson. Wilson, who lived with a white family near Yerington—hence his name—was a Paiute Indian. Despite his mundane identity, there would come a time when Jack Wilson would have fully a quarter of the people in the United States literally scared out of their wits.

It began innocently enough. In that year, a major eclipse of the sun occurred and coincidentally, young Jack Wilson was simultaneously stricken with a fever. Covered with sweat, he thrashed violently back and forth in his bed during the night. Strange sounds emanated from his throat.

When he awakened and the fever had subsided, Wilson told his astounded family that during the night, he had been taken to the afterworld. He had seen the Supreme Being. As the weeks passed and whites scoffed, more and more Indians came to hear the story of the strange dreamlike encounter.

Wilson's description never varied. He had been carried into the afterlife as if on a cloud, and there he had seen everyone who had died before him. It was as it had been for centuries. Both the young and the old engaged in ancient occupations, all frolicking together playing long-forgotten sports.

The tale was easy for most of Wilson's Indian friends to believe. At the time, few doubted that the white man had truly come to stay. But in the process of settling the west, the white man had destroyed nearly everything the Indians held dear; the pine nut trees, the rabbits, and the birds were gone.

The same thing held true in the east. All of the most powerful chiefs of the plains tribes had been either vanquished or banished. The buffalo, a staple of the red man's diet and lifestyle for centuries, had virtually disappeared. Most of the Indians who had decided to take advantage of the white man's "kindness" by living on the reservations provided for them, worked for slave-labor wages and food was scarce. Those who decided to reside elsewhere found freedom paid little more. For most, the end was near.

It was no wonder that the message of Wilson's dream fanned the tiny flames of hope. According to Wilson, the Supreme Being advised him to return to earth and lead his people along a path of peace with the whites, to devote themselves to work. If they followed the instruction and danced in a special ceremony, they would be reunited with the dead, the dead would be no more and the white man would disappear from the land forever. Said one white observer at the time, "It was a better religion than any they had before."

As representatives of the other tribes gathered to hear his story, Jack Wilson became known as Wovoka: spiritual leader.

The ceremony described by Wovoka was surprisingly simple, and every man, woman and child could participate. The worshippers donned red paint and shuffled slowly in a circle counter-clockwise. As the dance progressed, the tempo increased, and singers raised their voices in a song of resurrection.

Many who participated claimed to have fallen into a trance, that they had been transported to "paradise." They awoke to tell spine-tingling tales of conversations with lost ancestors. The spirits of the afterworld told of a new place where the buffalo would again roam free, where the white man never ventured.

The movement grew rapidly. Soon the preachings of Wovoka spread across the Great Plains, where they were embraced by the Arapaho, the Sioux, the Shoshone and the deadly Comanche. The Sioux even added a new twist. They adopted a bleached shirt of white muslin, on which symbols of the heavens, such as the sun and the moon, pictographs of earth and drawings of eagles and other birds of prey, were painted. Indian interpreters translated the garments into "Shirts of the Dead" or "Ghost Shirts." Soon rumors began to circulate among the whites. The shirts were bullet-proof, said frightened settlers.

The wearers of these shirts believed that they were invincible. A worried U.S. Army sent military observers. Indian Agent James McLaughlin summed up the situation in these words, "The infection has been so pernicious that many of our very best Indians appear dazed and undecided when talking of it."

By the summer of 1890, most of the western Indian tribes had taken up the teachings of Wovoka. Even the venerable Sitting Bull, whose fame had spread east from the Little Big Horn, had sent an emissary to Nevada, a believer known as Kicking Bear, to meet in private with Wovoka. Word of the meeting swept the territory. Now whites were more than simply worried. They were terrified.

There was good reason, of course, For those few whites willing to admit it, the lands of the Indian had been overrun, their wild game had been decimated and the white man's diseases—smallpox, malaria and the like—had swept through the reservations like wildfire, killing, by some estimates, more than 40 percent of the Indian population. Through it all, few, if any promises had been kept by "the Great White Father in Washington."

Suspicion and guilt met with tragedy on the Pine Ridge Reservation at Wounded Knee. After an attempt to enlist the services of Buffalo Bill Cody to lure Sitting Bull into a trap had failed, the army took the matter into its own hands. As the year of 1890 came to a close, 300 Indian men, women and children were massacred. Whites took up arms across the west. But to the Indian nation, it was seen as the last and most bitter defeat.

The Ghost Dance subsided quickly after the incident. Without further bloodshed, most Indians simply resigned themselves to the inevitable and refused to follow Wovoka further.

Wovoka himself, now disillusioned and weary, returned to Nevada and resumed his former identity under the name given to him by the Wilson family. The flame of hope for the Indians of North America flickered and died.

For a time, Jack Wilson had created a peaceful uprising in the fading American west. Some have called it a religious movement, others a "revitalization" of ancient beliefs. In any case, Wovoka, known to the whites as Jack Wilson, never dreamed again...

"The town of Elko is a considerable one, as towns go on the Humboldt Desert. The bright, white-painted hotel and the two or three neat stores and the station building have a thriving and busy look in the cheerful, early sunlight.

"The platform swarms with stalwart, bushy-bearded, long-booted natives, big hunting dogs loping along and clamorous representatives of the Shoshone nation...

"According to the guidebooks, Elko has a future as a watering place, boasting of six hot and cold mineral springs, one of which is agreeably known as the 'Chicken Soup Spring' and requires only pepper and salt and a willing imagination to make it a perpetual free soup kitchen. A bathhouse is already erected, and a large hotel is to follow which, it is confidently expected, will bring fashion and civilization by the carload into Elko.

—Leslie's Magazine—
1877

THEY CALLED HIM "DEATH VALLEY" SCOTTY...
-43-

Walter Scott was his name, but to most people, such as Nevada Governor Fred Balzar (he was the fella who signed the infamous bills making gambling and the 6 week divorce the state's main source of income), he was "Death Valley" Scotty, a true legend in his own time.

His antics were such that even popular American humorist Will Rogers referred to him from time to time in his syndicated column and on his national radio program. And for good reason. Nevada has had her share of characters, but for sheer audacity and pluck, "Death Valley" Scotty had them all beat hands down.

They called him "Death Valley" (some say wily Scott invented the moniker himself) after he made a series of prospecting forays out into the forbidding desert. Although he often met with little success, you wouldn't know it to hear Scotty tell it. Out there he had discovered a series of "rich" finds. Wherever he appeared, folks gathered round to hear him tell of the fame and fortune that was about to come his way.

There was a twinge of truth to almost every tale he told. The cagey prospector never seemed to come back to civilization empty handed, every sample contained specks of true gold. If nothing else, Scotty was a showman to rival the likes of P.T. Barnum. (In later years, most people wised up to Scotty. He had a habit of taking gold with him when he went out into the rugged terrain. If he failed to strike a vein, he simply brought his original samples back in with him, claiming another "big one" was right over the next horizon.)

Scotty was amazingly astute for a sourdough. He fully realized that finding a rich vein was only the beginning. Once a strike was located, hundreds of thousands of dollars were usually required to get at it. There were roads to be built, shacks, shanties and stamp mills. Food supplies, firewood and heavy equipment had to be dragged over some of the toughest terrain in the state. In other words, Scotty needed backers and he went to elaborate lengths to gain investors and credibility.

To establish himself as a fine and upstanding citizen, a man without prejudice in a rough frontier, he had his picture taken with a "heathen" Chinese, which made him a great favorite among the area's Oriental population. It mattered little to Scotty that he actually had owed the man money and was merely paying off an old debt.

Another time, he invited eastern investors to tour the site of his newest find, knowing full well that the location would yield little and that if the backers were able to examine the area closely, they would certainly realize the truth. No problem. Scotty just hired a few of his friends, dressed them up as Indians, and staged a mock attack on the group as they made their way out across the valley. The ruse worked, at least initially. The Easterners never did get close enough to examine his "discovery," but they were so mortified by the whole affair that they also refused to invest.

As a promoter, Scotty was unequaled. In July of 1925, he actually commandeered an entire train. You see, Scotty was bent on getting some more investors and the way he had it figured, the best way to attract attention was to make the national news.

He decided to rent a train and attempt to break the record for the run from Los Angeles to Chicago, and so he did. Depositing $4,000 with the Santa Fe Railroad, he held a press conference. He announced that he would pack the dining car with the finest goods and liquor that money could buy, that only his "friends" would ride along and that "a good time would be had by all!" As his piece de resistance, he even showed up at the depot in Los Angeles with a stray mutt under his arm. "I just gave this ol' dog a $1,000 collar," he exclaimed with a grin. "Now I'm gonna give him a little train ride." The comments and accompanying photos went out immediately over the national wire services.

The nation loved it. At every stop, reporters jammed the platforms and crowds pushed forward to wish him well. The trip itself was 2,265 miles. The record to beat: 53 hours. But "Death Valley" Scotty did it. He rolled into Chicago to a huge welcome in the record time of just under 45 hours. He had captured the country's imagination and lined up more than a few backers as

133

well.

But perhaps Scotty's greatest claim to fame was his famous "castle." Flushed with the success of his train ride, he decided to build a castle, smack dab in the middle of the desert.

Now such a wild idea was just another opportunity to Scott. He lined up a new investor, this time a Chicago tycoon, and a site was selected about 50 miles from Goldfield. By 1931, a sprawling ranch house, constructed entirely of native materials which were hauled over incredible stretches of wasteland, was in place. It covered an unbelievable 31,000 square feet and even featured a solar heating plant. (Remember, this was back in the 30's!) A lofty tower, complete with imported bell chimes, rose 50 feet in the air. There was even a spacious "guest" house for "visiting dignitaries."

But for all its grandeur, there was one small problem with Walter Scott's fabulous castle. It seems that he didn't own the property. The land on which his dream had been built was actually owned by the federal government. Officials, understandably, took a rather dim view of anyone, particularly the flamboyant. Scott, laying claim to government land.

The elegant lifestyle of "Death Valley" Scotty would soon come to an end. Although his early finds had yielded enough to make most men comfortable for life, later explorations were disappointing. Most of the gold he owned in his declining years was, wrote one historian, "primarily in his teeth." He died shortly thereafter in "his" castle on someone else's land.

"Death Valley" Scotty, was a prospector, con man and showman. He was both a rich man and a pauper. He built dreams from imagination and castles in the desert. Just the same, he became a legend. Before the end he was quoted as saying of his castle, "I like it out here. I'm living in the best damn place in town!"

Sadly, it should be noted, he was the only one there.

THE CHINESE: A CONFRONTATION ON THE COMSTOCK
-44-

The Chinese. Although few people would admit it at the time, they built the famous Transcontinental Railroad, providing the majority of the labor for the western section which wove its way up and over the Sierra Nevada Mountains.

Throughout the west, small "Chinatowns" sprung up, tiny ghettos where the Chinese could live and work in relative isolation and still be able to maintain the customs and traditions of their native land. They ran laundries, restaurants, and herb shops. If men were so inclined, an opium den was usually available, though whites seldom frequented them.

But it was tough going for the Chinese. Most Americans, the majority of which had been on this continent for less than a generation themselves, looked down their noses at the Orientals. Oh, they were alright to do the laundry; they were just fine if you needed some wood hauled, but other than that...

And things were particularly difficult on the Comstock. In Virginia City, the Chinese were, for the most part, tolerated, for they were excellent workers. They proved especially adept at gathering firewood, which was at a premium in the area due to the fact that almost every bush and tree had already been sacrificed to the earliest mining operations. With their patience and perseverance, they would scour the seemingly barren countryside, digging up stumps long since forgotten and chopping them into kindling. Backbreaking work to say the least.

For a time, things were quiet, but soon things came to a head in the mines, and silent persecution became open warfare. Fearing that the Chinese would work for a fraction of the wages afforded whites, the unions had steadfastly maintained regulations that prohibited the Orientals from working below the surface. But from time to time, angry confrontations occurred and armed miners would march on any operation where there was even a hint of the possibility of hiring Chinese.

The railroad, however, was another matter. Across the nation, inexpensive Chinese labor had allowed the giant rail barons to complete their lines in record time. They were not about to discontinue the practice. When the Virginia and Truckee Railroad, linking Virginia City with Reno and Carson City, was under construction, the Chinese built most of it with their sweat and blood.

But as the tracks approached the Comstock, the concern of the miners grew. Once the rails had been laid, they reasoned, what would prevent the Chinese from looking for work in the mines? Tension mounted. Daily there were incidents of harassment along the Divide. Chinese laborers were beaten, even shot at. The Orientals, who, for the most part, had not even considered working underground, continued to lay the rails closer and closer.

Finally, on October 7, 1869, Banker William Sharon decided something had to be done. Sharon held substantial interest in not only the railroad, but also the mines, and he feared that the miners would take the law into their own hands, bringing about a wholesale slaughter of the Chinese.

At six in the evening on October the 7th, Sharon mounted a platform at the hoisting works of the Yellow Jacket Mine in Gold Hill. For more than an hour, he regaled the hundreds of miners who had gathered with the concern and threat of Chinese labor and assured them that under no circumstances would the Orientals be allowed in the mines.

"I, too, have been a working man," said Sharon. "I have never intended to use the Chinese in the mines, but only for menial tasks, like railroad grading."

He went on to point out that his Bank of California was not the enemy, but the friend of labor. After all, he said, "What mine can be worked without capital?" As to the matter of Chinese labor on the railroad, he concluded, "The railroad will not only make supplies cheaper here on the Comstock, but it will allow the profitable milling of low-grade ore."

"Chinese were only used to grade railbeds because they worked cheaper," he continued. "Some of you recklessly assert that the white man could have been got to work as cheap, but everyman of you knows better than that!"

His oration proved successful and a reprisal against the Chinese was averted. By the time Sharon wound down, he was greeted with "Three Cheers for Mr. Sharon!"

Later in the evening, he spoke again, this time to the Virginia Miner's Union, and an agreement was drawn up that ended the matter once and for all. The Chinese would be allowed to work on the railroad below the American Mine in Gold Hill. After that, white workmen would take over. Under no circumstances, he again promised, would Orientals be permitted to work the mines. The crisis was finally over.

No Chinaman would ever be allowed to work underground, but, to the industrious Chinese, it hardly mattered. They continued to run many prosperous businesses in the area, all the while sending money to their homeland for safekeeping.

And when the mines of Virginia City began to peter out, most went west to San Francisco, where their "Chinatown" on the Barbary Coast became the largest oriental settlement of all.

"Through this canyon —untraveled even by a horseman before the rails of the Central Pacific Railroad —we pass the little town of Palisade, the tiniest of settlements, lodged between towering gray walls that cast a shadow over it even at noonday.

"A very short distance below is another nucleus of human life; a cluster of blackened and tattered teepees, around which lounge a few idle figures quite as aimless as brutes, and far dirtier. These are 'civilized Indians' —peaceable wards who live on their reservations or near them, with no greater object in life than to beg, steal, sleep and eat; and so far as the casual observer can see, not the slightest attempt is made to suggest any other aims to their minds...

—Frank Leslie's Illustrated Newspaper—
1877

THE CASE OF THE LIVELY CORPSE
-45-

He was found sitting upright at the dilapidated table, his beard flecked with tiny icicles, a light covering of frost adorning the top of his ancient head. On the table in front of him was a half-eaten plate of beans and a partial loaf of sourdough bread. Near his right hand was a cup of ice cold coffee.

A candle on a whiskey bottle had burned down and coated the table top with a small pool of wax. A torn pair of longjohns dangled forlornly from a bed post. A well-worn pick, propped up in the corner identified him as a prospector. A bullet mold on the cold forbidding hearth testified to the harshness of life on the frontier.

The scene was so lifelike it was eerie. But Old Hardtack was dead. He had succumbed to a heart attack, his body frozen stiff as a board.

Nevada winters sometimes come early and stay late. There was no way of knowing how long the lone prospector had been dead, for the cruel, biting cold had perfectly preserved the corpse. Old Hardtack sat upright in frozen splendor.

The cabin itself was a makeshift affair. Old newspapers filled the cracks in the walls. A gaping hole, where a window had been planned and never completed, covered instead with buckskin, greeted the rare passersby. In this rugged canyon some miles from the town of Pomeroy, it was unusual when anyone came by at all.

When the news of the prospector's demise was relayed by a drifter passing through, two men set out in a cutter sleigh to recover the body and bring it into town for burial in the spring. Arriving at the site after an arduous journey, the men discovered that the bitter cold and rigor mortis made "lyin' out the body" virtually impossible. Not wishing to unceremoniously dump the corpse in the rear of the sleigh, they decided to leave it in its sitting position. Tenderly, they placed Old Hardtack in the rear seat and wrapped a blanket around him. Now, not two, but three men began the long trip back down the mountain.

But the combination of the freezing cold and a frozen passenger made the living more than a little jumpy. As night approached, they decided to stop at a saloon and trading post to warm up a bit, to bolster their courage with a spot of whiskey.

The idea of sharing a sleigh with a dead man is a golden opportunity for story tellers. As the men warmed themselves before the roaring fire and the liquor began to take effect, the two regaled the other bar patrons with their tale of the lifelike corpse. Despite the inclement weather, most of the men couldn't resist the temptation to have a look, and out into the snow they trudged. All agreed. The corpse was certainly lifelike. And that gave a couple of pranksters an idea...

While the men from Pomeroy were warming to their whiskey, two others slipped out the back door and took the body of Old Hardtack from the sleigh. Stashing it carefully behind a nearby snowdrift, one of the men climbed aboard the sleigh and wrapped himself in the same blanket. He wouldn't have long to wait.

Now fortified, the Pomeroy men were ready to continue their journey. Bottle in hand, they set out once again for town.

Night had settled over the region and the only light was a lantern dangling precariously from the kick board. Ominous shadows leaped from the towering snowdrifts as the sleigh made its way slowly down the mountain.

As they began their final descent into Pomeroy, one of the men offered the precious bottle. "Care for a drink?" he asked his companion. "Don't mind if I do!" said the 'corpse' in the rear. The rest, as they say, is history.

The terrified men bailed out of the sleigh, leaving only the 'corpse' aboard. At the sound of their screams, the horses bolted and the now-careening vehicle thundered into town at breakneck speed.

The sheepish miners finally trudged into civilization on foot. At the saloon they were amazed to find the 'corpse' very much alive and toasting his practical joke along the bar. Drinks were on the house.

A prospector named Hardtack, even in death, had become a part of the Nevada legend.

SCHOOL OR SALOON?
THE CHOICE WAS CLEAR!
-46-

Battle Mountain. In its heydey it was a typical ripsnortin' frontier town, populated by railroaders and miners, ranchers, pimps, and prostitutes. And they all had one thing in common — a desire to somehow beat the system and get rich overnight. It was the timeless dream of every man.

And like every boomtown, Battle Mountain had its priorities, especially in terms of permanent structures. First, the town needed a saloon. After all, although there was plenty of romance attached to the dream of building a railroad or finding the big bonanza, the work itself was unbearably monotonous and backbreakingly hard. A saloon was a prerequisite to sanity, an unqualified "necessary evil."

Next came the church. Naturally when you have so much sinning going on in the saloon, you need a house of worship in which to repent, if no more frequently than every Sunday. So hot on the heels of the first saloon, the citizens of Battle Mountain followed, quite logically, with a church.

Next came a one-room schoolhouse. Regardless of the fact that less than 1% of the itinerant population was even capable of bearing a child, let alone raising one, it was considered a "civic duty" to provide a place of learning. The theory held that to attract serious investors, a new town had to bolster the impression that it was prepared for the onslaught of civilization, prepared to provide a worthy crop of future businessmen, ranchers and governors, and, with a little luck, even a senator or two.

There you have it, in order of importance -a saloon, a church and finally a school. All other permanent buildings -the hardware store, the livery, a courthouse, a jail, they could wait.

But as Battle Mountain continued to grow, so did the need for another saloon. Problem was: where to put it? It had to be convenient, somewhere near the center of town. Unfortunately the only choice piece of property left was right next to the new schoolhouse. The close proximity to inquiring minds didn't bother the saloonkeeper in the least. School or no school, he was determined to build a profitable watering hole. The next day hammers were flying and within a week a clapboard building had sprung up on the site.

Soon the children were having their study of "the three R's" punctuated by the sounds of raucous laughter, occasional fistfights and even a gunshot or two. It was getting pretty hard to teach readin', 'ritin', and 'rithmetic with guns going off in the air.

For the prim and proper schoolmarm, there was only one solution. She decided to take the matter directly to the city council. The choice was clear, she reasoned. The saloon simply had to go.

Sure enough, a meeting was held and the council listened closely to both sides of the case. The saloonkeeper testified that his right to operate ("Indeed the absolute right of every gallant citizen!") was the wish of the majority of Battle Mountain's lusty residents. The young schoolteacher testified that it would be impossible to instill in the children "an honest view of virtue, a civilized perspective of the goodness of man."

Tempers flared. The gavel pounded.

In the end, the council sided with the school teacher. They agreed that a school and a saloon simply could not exist side by side.

The following day the council of the city of Battle Mountain issued their decree. They ordered that the school be closed until a new schoolhouse could be built in a "more appropriate location."

Such were the priorities along the frontier.

"To call a place dreary, desolate, homeless, uncomfortable, and wicked is a good deal. We never found a place better deserving of the title than Virginia City.

—Mrs. Frank Leslie—
1877

THE V & T RAILROAD.
THEY SAID IT
COULDN'T BE DONE
-47-

Mother Nature is funny sometimes. Old timers, I'm sure, are probably convinced that she deliberately goes out of her way to make life difficult. For example, she gave Nevada one of the lowest annual rainfalls in the nation and then, damn, if she didn't put her richest ore supplies at the furthest point from water.

I'm convinced that Mother Nature simply has a little sense of humor. She must have chuckled when she decided on isolated Mount Davidson as the hiding place for the famous Comstock Lode. I can hear her now, "Just let them TRY to get supplies up here!"

Getting anything up the mountain was a problem. Every bit of food, lumber, and firewood, not to mention such essentials as whiskey, had to be hauled over terrain that could be called treacherous at best. Drivers were subjected to rock slides, runaway teams, highwaymen and bad weather. At times the wind blew so furiously that coaches warned passengers that they would be carried only "at your own peril!" In winter, the wind combined with heavy, drifting snow to halt all traffic for days at a time. It was not unusual for miners to find themselves stranded for weeks on end on the mountaintop, their only companion their desire for wealth.

The answer, of course, was a railroad. The steam locomotive was being touted as "the only way to travel!" It was big, strong, and could haul just about anything at less than half the price. Wagons took days to reach Virginia City. A steam engine could do the job in hours.

But more than a few of the men on the Comstock agreed with Mother Nature. It just simply couldn't be done. In some places, the grades would have to be 40 degrees. In other areas, the ground suddenly and mysteriously dropped away, sometimes hundreds of feet into unseen canyons.

But no matter how difficult the task, it was mutually agreed that a railroad was imperative. Supplies were needed desperately and a financially unstable country, still suffering from the aftereffects of a bloody Civil War, was trying to rebuild. Silver was the key. The nation anxiously awaited the seemingly inexhaustible storehouse of wealth stockpiled on the mountain. The rush to build a railroad began.

Five locomotives were ordered. Aptly named the Ormsby, the Lyon, the Storey, the Virginia and the Carson, contracts were drawn for immediate delivery. It was 1869 and still not a single foot of track had been laid.

But at the same time, 3,000 tons of rail was being loaded on a fleet of ships in the harbor of Liverpool, England. After five treacherous months at sea, they landed in San Francisco where the rails were quickly transferred to schooners bound for Sacramento. From there, the 6 million pounds of steel was loaded on wagons, then pulled by oxen over the towering Sierra. What "couldn't be done" was about to happen.

On September 28, Nevada's first locomotive was standing on a length of track hastily laid near the Carson City Mint. As crowds gathered and patriotic flags snapped bravely in the wind, Superintendent Yerington, newly installed as the head of the tiny Virginia and Truckee Railroad Company, wedged a silver spike, a gift from a Gold Hill assayer, in place and drove it home. It was a momentous occasion. As the city band struck up a lively tune, the lonely wail of a steam whistle broke the silence of the Valley for the first time. Livestock scattered in all directions.

By October 5, the rails stretched into the foothills. The following day the editor of the Carson Appeal reported that he had had the distinct pleasure of an observation ride accompanied by "ladies who rode precariously out on the cowcatcher." He also suggested that the time had come to "fence off the rangeland for fear that cattle would derail Nevada's pride and joy."

By November 13, 1869, the line was completed to the town of Gold Hill and every miner within 50 miles turned out to raise flags and glasses in salute. Mining and railroad magnate William Sharon was on hand to give the keynote address. The "impossible" had come true.

Today, of course, the V & T has faded into history. For more than 40 years she served faithfully the Comstock, the state and the nation. But with the closing of the mines and the decline in mineral wealth, her rails were abandoned to rust, her ties torn loose for firewood.

Thankfully you can still hear that lonesome wail up in Virginia City. Independent railroad buffs have run a short line back down the grade. Today you can climb aboard a steam engine and take a short trip back in time as the engineer entertains you with facts about her glorious past.

And who knows? Perhaps with some help, even more track will be laid. Perhaps some day the V & T will ride the rails once again here in Nevada.

For many, that day can't come too soon...

DON'T HANG
JOHN MILLAENIN!
-48-

By nine in the morning of April 24, 1868, the streets of Virginia City were bustling with activity. The mood of the crowds of milling spectators was one of anticipation, of excitement. A man was about to be hung.

Not any man, mind you, but the murderer of Julia Bulette.

Although a mere prostitute, Julia Bulette had become, quite literally, a legend in her own time. Virginia City residents had always prided themselves on the frontier philosophy of "live and let live," and Bulette had become a sterling example of this progressive thinking, having succeeded in advancing the world's oldest profession to startling new heights.

She was the first to bring the "trade" out of the closet and into the light of day. She could walk the streets in broad daylight (no pun intended —it was a luxury unheard of at the time), without a whisper or a hint of scorn. She even became an honorary member of Engine Company No. 1, Virginia's most prestigious volunteer fire brigade, a tribute usually accorded only visiting politicians and high-ranking businessmen. Even more surprising was the fact that she had a few close friends among the leading ladies of society.

When news of her violent death became known the entire Comstock was enraged. It was one thing to kill a man on the frontier. In fact shootings and the like were common at the time. But it was quite another to take advantage of a woman, regardless of her "profession."

Her body had been found disheveled, spread out across her bed. There were marks around her delicate throat, indications that a pillow had been pushed down over her face. There was a small hole in her forehead. Signs of a struggle were everywhere.

In every saloon and business, the topic of conversation was the same. Angry voices were raised, encouraging the formation of a committee of vigilantes. Lynching was on the minds of everyone and blood was in the air.

Within weeks, a man by the name of John Milleanin was brought to trial. The evidence was purely circumstantial, but damning nevertheless. He had sold a dress that had belonged to the murdered woman. Bulette had purchased it just shortly prior to her death. An inspection of his room turned up additional articles which had belonged to the victim.

An endless stream of witnesses paraded for the prosecution. Milleain, however, was not so fortunate. A Frenchman who spoke little English, he was unable to find a single person who would testify in his behalf.

The outcome of the trial was predictable. The jury deliberated little more than a hour before bringing in a decision. Although they filed back into the courtroom well after midnight, church bells rang out along the Comstock Lode when the verdict was announced. Revenge, thought many, was finally within reach. Milleanin was escorted back to his jail cell.

But soon the murderer began to have visitors. Within the next few days, women from along the Comstock dropped by, bringing flowers for his cell and an assortment of homemade pies, cakes and candies. Some of the wives of the town's most upstanding citizens showed up to console the prisoner in his final hours.

It helped, of course, that the Frenchman was a handsome devil. More importantly, perhaps, was the fact that although Julia Bulette had been tolerated by the women of Virginia City for years, these women now saw a chance to make a statement for themselves. It was good riddance to bad rubbish, they said. They wrote letters to the condemned man. Perfumed hankerchiefs were delivered to the jail.

But the outpouring of feminine sympathy did little to sway the male majority. At precisely twelve o'clock on the 24th, the prisoner stepped out the door of the Sheriff's office and boarded a carriage for the execution site. As tearful women watched from curtained windows, a flatbed wagon followed. In it rode an undertaker with a coffin.

Almost 5,000 people turned out to witness the execution, including a sizeable number of women and children. The gallows, consisting of two uprights and a crossbeam some 16 feet high, was situated in a sloping ravine about a mile northeast of the city, just below present-day Geiger Grade and near the Jewish burial ground.

"Arriving at the scaffold," wrote reporter Dan DeQuille, "the prisoner ascended with a light tripping step, and now stood boldly forth and took a last look upon whom were once his fellow citizens and who were now assembled to see him take his final leap into the dark." Women began to weep.

Milleanin read his final words in French from handwritten sheets of paper. For more than ten minutes he continued in a calm voice, accusing the Sheriff of perjury and the prosecution of parading "abandoned women" in to testify. He maintained his innocence to the end.

At ten minutes to one the trap was sprung and the door disappeared from beneath John Milleanin. A gasp rose from the crowd and then a hush fell over the hillside. The body twirled slowly in the afternoon sun for a full 25 minutes before it was cut down and tossed unceremoniously into the waiting coffin.

John Milleanin, convicted murderer of Julia Bulette, prominent citizen and popular prostitute, was dead.

"It is a good thing, too," remarked a bystander. "If the city hadn't kilt him, we sure as hell would!"

"How Long Will It Last?"

"A supply of partially pulverized ore shoots, like a lot of small coal for stove use, down a shaft. It is falling into a bucket by the side of which stands a man who is prepared to carry it away when it is full. The supply of ore seems inexhaustible, and this raises the important question: 'How long will it last?'

No other discovery has ever created half so much excitement as this famous ore body. Soon the telegraph wire had spread the important news around the world, and the most exciting anticipations were formed as to its present and future. Some experts have estimated the value of the ore body at not less than $1,700,000,000...

—Frank Leslie's Illustrated Newspaper—
1877
The writer was referring to the fabulous Comstock Lode

RUSTLER'S PUNISHMENT
-49-

If you were planning to become a rustler in early Nevada, it was a good idea to take your profession seriously. You see, rustling required timing, planning and, quite naturally, a certain degree of intelligence. Unfortunately, two fellows named Ruspas and Reese seemed to lack all three of these characteristics.

It happened near the shores of Washoe Lake, just north of Genoa, the state's first permanent settlement. At the time, the area was sparsely populated. There were a few ranchers, some three dozen farms and even a few small businesses. The real rush to Washoe and the fabulous silver booms were still a few more years in the future.

It was natural, then, that two strangers entering the valley with a yoke of healthy oxen for sale would cause quite a stir. Curiosity peaked when the locals learned that the two men wanted to sell the critters at a fraction of their worth. Though most of the ranchers were suspicious, oxen were rare and highly prized in the region. Men rode in from miles around to inspect the animals firsthand.

The oxen were fat and sassy, obviously well-cared for. They showed no signs of the long and arduous ordeal of crossing the plains, the route along which Ruspas and Reise claimed they had traveled.

And Ruspas and Reise didn't look like settlers, either. At least not the kind that looked like they were headed for California. Far from acting like homesteaders, the two men were unkempt, with hair to shoulder length. Their hands were soft, not hardened by years of back-breaking agricultural chores. To top things off, both men claimed to be single and, as everyone knew, no farmer worth his salt would try to homestead without the help of a wife.

So the two men became the hot topic of conversation in the valley. Wasn't it strange, some said, that the oxen were in such

148

good shape? Wasn't it kind of funny that the men were asking such a low price? What kind of settler had no wife? Could it be...could it be that the oxen had been stolen?

Word traveled fast. Within a few days, a deputy had located a Dayton rancher by the name of Campbell. Sure enough, a prized ox team had been stolen from his ranch. Returning to Washoe Lake, the Deputy quickly took Ruspas and Reise into custody.

I know you've probably heard all the stories about early Nevada justice; how a rustler caught was usually a rustler hung, and hung from the nearest cottonwood tree. No trial, no pleading, no judge or jury. Just bring up a wagon, throw a rope over the nearest branch and that was it —a lesson to all who refused to walk the straight and narrow. The Code of the West.

Actually, that was rarely the case in Nevada.

A trial, such as it was, was held for Ruspas and Reise. It convened under a large pine tree on the shore of the lake. The jury consisted of many of the same local farmers and ranchers who had inspected the stolen oxen when the team had first been offered for sale. Though Ruspus and Reise pleaded "not guilty" and stuck to their story, it was no use. Campbell positively identified his stolen oxen. Ruspus and Reise were convicted of rustling in less than an hour.

Instead of hanging, however, it was decided that the two men should be banished from the territory. But as the rustlers began to breath a sigh of relief, the jury foreman continued. There would be another condition of freedom. Each man would have his left ear cut off. It would serve as a permanent reminder of their indiscretion, a sign to all that rustling in Nevada would never be tolerated.

The jury drew lots and a man named Sturtevant was chosen to carry out the sentence. Dutifully, he drew his knife and sliced off the left ear of Reise, tossing it ceremoniously to the rest of the jury. Slowly he moved toward Ruspus.

But when he pulled back the outlaw's long hair, a gasp went up from the men. Ruspus was already missing his left ear! Apparently, he had been caught in a similar situation once before. The jury hastily reconvened.

After some more deliberation it was decided that "a verdict was a verdict." An ear had to go, regardless of the fact that Ruspas had only one remaining. Sturtevant promptly disposed of the other ear.

The two men were allowed some doctoring and then released. They were ordered to head west into California and warned never again to return to the Washoe Valley. Under the watchful eyes of two deputies, they were escorted to the foothills of the Sierra.

History does not record what became of the two inept rustlers, but the amount of rustling declined dramatically over the next decade despite the lawlessness of the region.

The badmen had gotten the message. Steal in Nevada and, though you might escape the hangman, you could very well lose an ear.

Funny. I know of some people who think we should return to those days again...

THEY NAMED IT AFTER RENO
-50-

In doing the research for this book, from time to time I have used the lazy man's approach. You see, I learned a long time ago that the most interesting historians of any age are to be found not beneath a stack of musty books at the local library. Rather, they are real people with other vocations who were actually there and remember how it really was, people who, at the very least, have an old book, a newspaper, a diary or possibly a letter with which to prove it.

This is certainly not to say that diligent research is not a noble profession. Far from it. But I have found that true history is a lot like that elusive outcropping of gold for which we are always searching; most of it lies buried well below ground, hidden ingeniously from prying eyes. You never know what is there until you start to dig.

In much the same manner, many of the true facts about the Silver State lie buried still, waiting silently perhaps in someone's attic, waiting patiently for someone to discover them again.

In the course of my usual speaking engagements, I have been asking people to go through some of their most cherished possessions in hopes of finding something new about Nevada, something never published before.

The response has been excellent, but the procedure has its drawbacks. For every piece of information I receive, I'm also forced to give up some of my own. To be perfectly truthful, retelling some stories becomes downright tiresome after a while.

For example, I'm tired of explaining to people how Reno got its name. Was it named after the famous Major who almost made it to the Little Bighorn? Was it named for someone else? How did the selection come about? Well, I'm going to lay to rest the naming of Reno, Nevada, once and for all.

151

It was 1866 when word reached the tiny settlement of Lake's Crossing on the Truckee River that a railroad was on the way. For years there had been talk of plans to link the east and west by rail, but few took the rumors seriously. There was a recent Civil War for one thing, and the country was destitute. There was also another little obstacle called the Sierra Nevada Mountains.

But there was one person in the Truckee Meadows who believed. His name was Myron Lake and he was the owner, literally, of that little community. The place consisted of a bridge, a hotel, a grist mill, a kiln, a livery and a few other outbuildings. Five years earlier, in 1861, Lake had purchased some property at the best ford in the Truckee River, constructed a toll bridge, and within a few short seasons, he had become a prosperous man.

It has been said that some people are just plain lucky, that they are always in the right place at the right time. If true, Myron Lake was a perfect example. Shortly after the construction of his first bridge, a torrent of humanity was headed toward the fabulous Comstock Lode. For the vast majority of these prospectors, the only way to get there was across Lake's little bridge —for a fee, of course.

By 1866, Myron Lake was convinced that the coming of the railroad was more than just idle speculation. For the past year, four California backers —Charles Crocker, Leland Stanford, Mark Hopkins and Collis Huntington, had put together the necessary financing. They had brought in an Oriental work force as well, men who would work for low wages and weren't familiar with that discouraging phrase, "It simply can't be done!"

On December 13, 1867, the word that Lake had been anxiously awaiting finally arrived. The first locomotive cleared the treacherous pass and was steaming onto the valley floor. Although almost a full year would pass before the tracks would reach Lake's Crossing, Myron Lake knew that he was about to become wealthier still.

He put his plan to get in on the action into motion. He first cultivated a relationship with Charles Crocker, the only one of the "Big Four" to devote continuous interest to the project. He suggested to Crocker, ever open to a good deal, that he would be willing to donate 400 acres of land to the railroad. All the railroad had to do was agree to locate its depot on the property, which, quite incidentally, happened to adjoin Lake's bridge. Crocker, anxious to boast of an "instant railhead," was quick to accept.

By the summer of 1868, an agreement had been reached. Under its terms, Crocker received the land which he promptly divided up into 400 choice lots, 127 of which he immediately turned back over to Lake. Construction of a depot was soon under way. All that remained was to rename the new station. Crocker had stubbornly contended that the name, though it perpetuated the birthright of his new business associate, just wouldn't do. It was too long for one thing, too long to print on railroad timetables, and too difficult for passengers to hear over the clatter of wheels on steel. Instead, Crocker suggested the name of Jesse Reno.

Reno, whose family name had been anglicized from the French "Renault," had never been to the area. In fact, he had never even been west. Also, he was dead. He had been killed from ambush near a place called South Mountain, Maryland, during the Civil War. Just the same, "Reno" was easy to say. It was short and sweet and conductors could get the message across without missing a beat. Lake's Crossing became Reno. That was the way Charley Crocker wanted it. The year was 1868.

Wrote the Carson City Appeal, "Reno has sprung up feathered and lively. (Carson) must not let the new city on the Truckee run away with the capitol one of these days."

But Crocker was not a man to take chances. He was determined to make sure that his new railhead would enjoy a steady rate of growth. He offered 50 acres of land to the family of the first child born in Reno. The following article soon appeared in the Virginia City Territorial Enterprise. "First birth in Reno! Today is recorded the birth of a daughter. The happy father, J.A. Carnahan, formerly of Virginia City, concluded to change his residence and having established himself, set out to do what any good citizen would do toward the advancement and improvement of the town. His 9-pound daughter is the first child born in the place and takes the real estate." The paper alluded subtly to the fact that Carnahan had moved to Reno shortly before the birth and that Reno itself would never amount to much without such growth incentives.

There.

Now, no more questions about how Reno got its name, o.k.?

"In making slapjacks a miner considers himself a greenhorn if he is not able to turn them without doing it with a knife. He shuffles the cake about in the pan until it is loosened, then deftly tosses it into the air, catching it, batter side down, as it descends.

"I have heard of men who could throw a slapjack up through the chimney, then run outside of the house and catch it before it struck the ground, but I have never had the good fortune to see the feat performed...

—Comstock reporter Dan DeQuille—
circa 1876

TRUTH IN ADVERTISING THINGS HAVEN'T CHANGED A BIT!
-51-

Commercials.

Though I've been writing them for a lot of years, I can honestly say I have never written one that began with the words "We surveyed 1,000 doctors..." or "Do you suffer from..(pick any one of the following, it doesn't matter)...hemorrhoids?...lower back pain?...Athlete's foot?...that achy, nagging feeling?"

Never have. And I'm proud of it. You see, I know that research can be pushed and pulled, stretched and pummeled. If you try hard enough, you can usually create just the kind of results you've been looking for. For that reason, I don't believe half of those commercials. Do you?

Today, of course, things are different. Today we're protected by something called "Truth in advertising," a clever little law that keeps false or misleading statements away from our tender little minds. Everything we see, hear or read about today's products is true.

If you believe that, I have a nice hunk of Death Valley real estate I'd like to sell you.

Deceptive advertising isn't new, of course; it's been around since the dawn of time. Here in Nevada, for example, an edition of the Winnemucca Silver State, dated 1881, ran the following:

> "A person is prematurely old when
> balding occurs before the 45th year.
> Use Hall's Hair Renewer. Only Hall's
> can keep your scalp healthy and
> prevent baldness."

Sound familiar? It should. There are more than a dozen products, including one that is featured on an entire hour of cable television programming, that promise the very same thing.

154

Here's an ad for a product that no longer exists today though the language used is still turning up more than 100 years later:

"For 30 years, Brown's Bronchial
Troches have been recommended by
physicians the world over and has
always given perfect satisfaction.
A cough, cold or sore throat should
be stopped, for neglect can
frequently result in consumption
and incurable lung disease. Brown's
Troches do not disorder the stomach
like cough drops. Brown's Troches
act directly on the inflamed parts
to cure the irritation."

Recognize the phrases, "recommended by physicians," "doesn't upset your stomach," and "acts directly on the inflamed area?" Somehow, things never seem to change.

Think the "Money Back Guarantee" is a new idea, dreamed up by some young Madison Avenue type with a beard and tons of gold chains? Not at all. An 1882 advertisement for Bucklen's Arntex Salve:

"The best salve in the world for
cuts, bruises and sores. Cures
ulcers, salt rheum, chilblains,
corns and all kinds of skin
eruptions. 25 cents a box. This
salve is guaranteed to give
perfect satisfaction in every
case or your money will be
cheerfully refunded."

See?

One of my favorite cons ran on June 3, 1881. Like so many of our modern ads, this one hardly looked like an advertisement at all. It was placed squarely in the middle of a column of news stories disguised under the heading "Woman's Wisdom."

"She insists that it is of
more importance that her family
shall be kept in full health than

155

that she should have all the
fashionable dresses and styles
of the times. She therefore
sees to it that each member of
her family is supplied with
enough Hop Bitters at the first
appearance of any sign of ill
health, to prevent a fit of
sickness, with its attendant
expense, care and anxiety. All
women should exercise their
wisdom this way."

(I can hear me now, trying that one on my wife, "No, dear. You can't have a new dress. We need to stock up on Bitters...")

How many times have you heard the word "new" used with products?

"At a time when the community
is flooded with so many unworthy
devices and concoctions, isn't
it refreshing to find one that
is so beneficial and pure? So
conscious are the proprietors
of Dr. King's Discovery for
consumption that now it is
NEW AND IMPROVED!!!"

Not content to take any chances on losing the reader's attention, Dr. King even combined "new and improved" with the old "free sample" concept:

"The makers offer a trial
bottle FREE OF CHARGE! This
certainly would be disastrous
to them did not the remedy
possess the remarkable curative
qualities claimed. Dr. King's
new discovery for consumption
will POSITIVELY cure asthma,
bronchitis, stubborn coughs,
colds, phthsic, quinsy, horseness,

croup, or any other affection of
the throat or lungs."
Powerful stuff, huh?

"As you value your very existence,
give this wonderful remedy a try
by calling W.F. Stevens, druggist,
and obtain a trial bottle free of
cost or a regular size bottle for
a mere $1.00."

Aha! They even had those little sample bottles that clutter up your mailbox today.

Yep, nothing has really changed in the world of advertising in more than a century. Back around the time those ads were running in early Nevada newspapers, a fella by the name of P.T. Barnum was making quite a name for himself in other parts of the country. Although he never actually said "There's a sucker born every minute," he was smart enough to know that if you bent the truth a little, somebody was bound to believe it.

That sad but true philosophy is still around today...

Say, doesn't Joe Isuzu remind you of a snakeoil salesman...?

THE NEWSPAPER MAN
-52-

Old newspapers were colorful, at time downright bawdy.

They were sometimes factual, often not.

But one thing was certain: the old papers were the mirror image of the men who ran them.

The local editor was, at times, a reporter, a preacher, and, above all, the moral conscience of the community rolled into one. I would have given anything to have been a newspaperman back in Nevada's early days, especially if I could have been a fella like Sam Davis.

Davis got his start as a reporter on the Comstock. He was a practical joker of the first order. For example, when he became the editor of the Carson Appeal several years later, he often used humor to boost circulation and solve the newspaper's problems as well, as he did when he created the fictitious Wabuska Mangler.

There was the time he was having trouble collecting a bill owed him by Doc Benton, a prominent physician. Seems that the good doctor owed practically everyone in town, Sam included. Sam, however, decided to do something about it.

Learning that Benton was in Sacramento, California, on business, Davis printed a story claiming that Benton was actually enjoying himself at a race track. He went on to mention casually that Benton had "made a killing." He added slyly that "Doc will be returning to Carson City flush with his winnings on the afternoon stage."

Sure enough, the following day, Doc Benton returned to the state capitol, sitting proudly up beside driver Hank Monk. But what he saw astounded him. There, lining both sides of the street, was half the town, waving and cheering frantically as if he was some sort of conquering hero. Doc turned smartly to the thunderous applause and doffed his hat to the milling throng.

But when Doc finally dismounted, he learned to his dismay that the huge "welcoming" party was not made up of friends and acquaintances, but bill collectors. As the townspeople pressed forward, palms extended, Benton dipped into his satchel and paid off the crowd.

The ruse had worked brilliantly. Sam Davis, and most of the town's creditors, received their money.

Such shenanigans were typical of Davis. In his view, the newspaper was there for him to use as he saw fit. And use it he did.

But a practical joker can often become the butt of practical jokes as well. Once, when Sam had openly poked fun at a group of prominent businessmen in Virginia City, they decided to give him a taste of his own medicine. They decided to get even.

They began by convincing Sam that he should enter politics. They somberly advised him to throw his "considerable resources" behind the campaign of a local barber, named R.T. Brodek, who was running for the office of County Coroner. If Brodek were to win the election, Sam was told, Sam himself would soon become the Deputy Coroner.

This was music to the ears of the veteran newsman. The Coroner, he knew, was always in the thick of things. If a shooting, stabbing or a murder took place, who would be the first to know about it? What better way to stay on top of things than to become a part of the Coroner's office?

Sam was hooked. He immediately threw the power of the press into the fray. He himself stomped the sagebrush for Brodek. He even dipped into his own pocket for campaign financing.

Sure enough, his efforts paid off. Brodek won the election easily and the next day Sam hurried to his office to claim his appointment.

It was then that he learned that the tables had been turned on him. Sam would not be appointed Deputy Coroner, and for a very good reason. He couldn't be. There was no law on the books allowing the Coroner to appoint anyone, let alone a Deputy. While he laughed along with the rest of Carson City, Sam Davis knew he had fallen for the oldest trick of all.

Davis, however, would go down in our history as one of the most honest, energetic editors of his day. He was kind, generous almost to a fault, and always he maintained a sense of humor and a fierce pride.

I thought about that pride the other day when I came across one of his little-known writings. Whenever he came upon an interesting news item or just happened to make an observation, he frequently scribbled his thoughts on whatever happened to be handy.

What follows is a perfect example. It was penned on the back of a piece of butcher paper one evening as he returned from work. No one knows what prompted Sam to jot down such intense feelings about the Silver State, but I think his love of Nevada is shared by many who live here today...

Have you ever scented the sagebrush
That mantles Nevada's plain?
If not, you have lived but half your life
And that half lived in vain...

No matter where the place or clime
Your wandering footsteps stray,
You sigh as you think of her velvet fields
And their fragrance of leveled hay.

You will loiter a while in other lands
When something seems to call,
And the lure of the sagebrush calls you back
And holds you in its thrall.

You may tread the halls of pleasure
Where the lamps of folly shine,
Mid the sobbing of sensuous music
And the flow of forbidden wine.

But when the revel is over
And the dancers turn to go,
You will long for a draught of her crystal streams
That spring from her peaks of snow.

You will sigh for a sight of the beetling crags
Where the storm king holds his sway,
Where the sinking sun with its brush of gold,
Tells the tale of the dying day.

And when you die you will want a grave
Where the Washoe Zephyr blows.
With the green of the sagebrush above your head,
What need to plant the rose...

To the words of Sam Davis, I would only add "Amen".

THE PAST REMEMBERED
-52-

This year I have been trying little experiment. Whenever I give a speech, time permitting, I have tried to add a Q & A session at the end, and have added a few questions of my own. Namely, "What events do you remember most?" and "What happenings of vital importance stick out in your mind"? The answers came from people ranging up to 92 years of age. Their remembrances provide a keen insight into the true history of the State of Nevada.

THE KLONDIKE GOLD RUSH - 1900: In the two years after gold was discovered just over the border of what is now Alaska, more than 60,000 prospectors, many of them from Nevada, hit the trail north. There was a tremendous exodus from the Silver State that worried those who stayed behind.

THE SAN FRANCISCO EARTHQUAKE - 1906: the greatest earthquake in US history was followed by a horrific fire which engulfed the financial capitol of western America. Half the city was left homeless, the flames stretching for miles across the fabled hills along the Bay. Here in Nevada, the state's mining industry trembled as well. Though Nevadans sent thousands of dollars to aid the stricken city, panic closed the stock exchanges of Tonopah, Goldfield and the boomtowns. More than a few Nevadans saw the wealth they had accumulated during the days of the Comstock Lode consumed in the blaze.

THE MODEL T IS BORN - 1910: Henry Ford's first Model T rolled off the assembly line. It seated two people and cost an extravagant $850.00. While at first sales were sluggish, many were brought to Nevada immediately. They were found to be faster and more comfortable for mining exploration than the mule. The Old West was beginning to disappear.

MARK TWAIN DIES - 1910: Many Nevadans still considered Twain a favorite son when he passed away in Danbury, Connecticut.

Although he had spent but a decade here and was not particularly well-liked during the period, Nevadans had followed his exploits around the world. Halley's Comet, visible here in Nevada, appeared at the time of his death. Ironically, it had also passed over the state when he was born.

THE JOHNSON-JEFFRIES PRIZE FIGHT - 1910: This fight put Reno, Nevada on the map. The city had been struggling to retain its identity after the decline of the mining industry near Virginia City. Champion Johnson's victory over the white contender Jim Jeffries sparked a series of racial riots across the country. In Reno, 8 negroes were reported killed. Still, so popular was the bout that more than 20,000 spectators poured into the city to witness the event. It was the first Nevada "special event" to attract world-wide attention.

THE US ENTERS WW1 - 1917: Nevadans had followed the events our own Civil War and confrontations across the sea, but this was the first real conflict in which Nevadans truly marched off to the front in significant numbers. The male population of the state was seriously depleted. It was reported that after declaring war, members of Congress stood and cheered. President Wilson returned to the White House and wept, saying "My message was one of death for young men. How odd it seems to applaud that..."

PROHIBITION! - 1920: On January 16, the sale of beer, wine and liquor was officially banned by the 18th Amendment to the Constitution. In New York City, officers estimated that it would take a police force of more than 250,000 men to control the situation. In Nevada, most bars simply ignored the law. Nevadans went right on drinking.

TELEVISION ARRIVES - 1926: A new machine capable of the wireless transmission of moving images was unveiled in London by Scottish inventor M. John Baird. Many Nevadans remembered reading about it, but few believed it was possible. It would be 40 more years before the device would take hold in the state.

THE STOCK MARKET TUMBLES - 1929: Actually, it crashed with a rumble that shook the financial structure of the entire state. Known as Black Thursday throughout the rest of the country, it signaled the beginning of a longer-term disaster for Nevada which had prospered, though precariously, up until that time. Nevada's largest chain of banks would eventually close.

163

BOULDER CITY CREATED BY FEDS - 1930

When the Boulder Canyon Project, an act which resulted in the creation of Hoover Dam, was signed into law in 1928, the tiny town of Las Vegas was ecstatic, for it expected to grow by leaps and bounds. But the Federal Government. After all, Las Vegas had a redlight district, and it had openly defied prohibition. So the government decided to build a town of its own and did. Boulder City was to be a "wholesome, new, American" community. To keep strict moral control, the site was made a federal reservation where state laws did not apply. The government decided how many could live there, which business would be allowed, even what kinds of shrubs would be planted.

It was the first truly "planned community" in the United States. Soon the miraculous Hoover Dam, the "greatest feat of engineering in history" would bridge the raging Colorado River. During the Great Depression, it was one of the few places in the country that offered employment.

GAMING/DIVORCE BILLS PASSED - 1932: Nevada Governor Fred Balzar killed two birds with one stone and set a course for the state that continues to this day. The first law created a six-week waiting period for a divorce which molded an image that present-day Nevadans abhor. The second legalized gambling, leading to a tax-free prosperity that many states are now copying.

SOCIAL SECURITY LAW ENACTED - 1935: President Roosevelt signed into law an Act which advocated "Freedom from want in old age." Few in Nevada believed him.

WAR OF THE WORLDS - 1938: Americans nationwide panicked when Orson Welles made his famous radio broadcast on Halloween. There were traffic jams along the east coast as many Easterners just packed up all their belongings and headed for safety. Phone lines across the country were jammed with inquiries. Here in Nevada, perhaps because there was only one full-time radio station, most people just slept through it all. The following morning, Nevadans joked about the "foolishness" of the rest of the nation.

INDUSTRIAL COMPLEX CREATED - 1941:
The United States had the plans. They had been smuggled out of Nazi Germany by British spies. Now the government decided to look for a location to manufacture a new type of explosive. The Basic Magnesium Complex was created outside of Las Vegas.

Even today it remains the state's only concentration of heavy industry.

JAPANESE BOMB PEARL HARBOR - 1941: The attack on the US Naval Base in Hawaii stunned the entire country. The panic was particularly acute in the western states which bordered on the Pacific Coast. Many Nevada men signed up immediately, leaving a shortage of dealers in the gambling halls. The situation would give rise to women dealers for the first time. The war itself would introduce troops, either passing through to the front or returning home, their first glimpse of legalized gambling. In Las Vegas, war shortages would hamper gangster Bugsy Siegal's building plans for his new Flamingo Hotel, though only temporarily.

ROOSEVELT DIES! - 1945: The nation's 31st president had been popular in Nevada. Elaborate funeral services were held throughout the state. Sadly, Roosevelt never lived to see the end to World War II though it was just around the corner.

ATOM BOMB DROPPED ON HIROSHIMA! - 1945: Many Nevadans were aware of atomic testing in New Mexico and parts of Nevada, but few imagined the awesome power of the bomb. It would mark the end of WWII and servicemen, many of whom were discharged on the west coast flush with combat pay, headed immediately to the gambling halls of Nevada to celebrate. It would signal a new era of prosperity for an economically faltering state.

THE ATOM BOMB - 1951

President Truman had been reluctant to continue atomic testing within the borders of the continental United States, but the Korean War changed all that. On January 27, 1951, Las Vegans awoke to a fireball in the desert sky. It was the first test at the new Nevada Proving Ground.

Nevadans embraced the bomb. There were mushroom cloud hairdos and Atom Bomb cocktails. Retail stores offered Atom Bomb Sales. Though scientists in white garb actually interviewed residents on the city's streets, people were told that very little danger existed.

About Whom Great Stories are Told...

The major events that native Nevadans remember most, perhaps will come as a surprise to readers from other parts of the country. While each event has had a profound effect on the State -on our growth, our national status, on the way that we think and feel, we sound very much like any other region.

In reality, Nevada is a far cry from the image of cowboys and Indians, of gandy dancers and card sharks. We are a state just coming into its own.

It should be remembered that a people can be fairly judged only against the background of their own time. The western frontier was a place of hard work and hardship. It was particularly so here in the desert. Despite the image of sin which has plagued us since the first silver strike, most Nevadans attended church regularly. Those who did not stood little chance of success in business. Despite of image of divorce, we marry much more frequently, and stay that way. Despite our reputation as gamblers, that industry paves our roads and teaches our children.

Our land has been crossed and recrossed by explorers, trappers, prospectors, settlers and now tourists. Few have left more than footprints. But today we can see the results of the labors of those who have come to stay —our cities and towns, no matter how glitzy or quaint, how metropolitan or isolated, stand tall as monuments to their tenacity.

The men and women who have built Nevada are the kind of folks about whom great stories are told.

I will continue to tell them as long as these old fingers hold out......

Bibliography

Angel, Myron, *History of Nevada 1881*, Burbank: Howell-North Books, 1858

Bryant, Edwin, *What I Saw In California*, Lincoln: University of Nebraska Press, 1985

Curran, Harold, *Tearful Crossing: The Central Overland Trail Through Nevada*, Reno: Nevada Publications, 1982

DeQuille, Dan (William Wright), *The Big Bonanza*, Reno: Nevada Publications, 1974

Doten, Alfred, *The Journals of Alf Doten 1849-1903*, Walter Van Tilburg Clark, ed, Reno: University of Nevada Press, 1973

Drury, Wells, *An Editor on the Comstock Lode*, Palo Alto: Pacific Books, 1948

Earl, Phillip I., *This Was Nevada*, Nevada Historical Society, Reno: University of Nevada Press, 1986

Edward, Jerome E., *Pat McCarran, Political Boss of Nevada*, Reno: University of Nevada Press, 1982

Endoes, Richard, *Saloons of the Old West*, Salt Lake City: Howe Brothers, 1985

Glasscock, Carl B., *Gold in Them Hills*, Las Vegas: Stanley Pahler, 1988

Higgs, Gerald B., *Lost Legends of the Silver State*, Salt Lake City: Western Epics Publishing Company, 1976

Lewis, Oscar, *Silver Kings*, Reno: University of Nevada Press, 1986

—*The Town That Died Laughing*, Reno: University of Nevada Press, 1986

Nielson, Norm, *"Tales of Nevada!"*, Fun and Gaming Magazine, 1986, 1987, 1988, 1989.

—*"Tales of Nevada!"* radio scripts: Nos. 61 through 1404.

—*Reno: The Past Revisited*, Norfolk: Donning Company, 1988

Pahler, Stanley W., *Mark Twain in Virginia City*, Las Vegas: Nevada Publications, 1985
—*Nevada Ghost Towns and Mining Camps*, Berkeley: Howell-North Books, 1970
—*Nevada Towns and Tales: North, Vol 1*, Reno: Nevada Publications, 1981
—*Nevada Towns and Tales: South, Vol 2*, Reno: Nevada Piblications, 1982
Rice, George Graham, *My Adventures With Your Money*, Las Vegas: Nevada Publications, 1986
Sengstacken, Agnes, *Destination West*, Portland: Binsfords and Mort, 1942
Stratton, Joanna L., *Pioneer Women*, New York: Simon and Shuster, 1981
Taylor, Jock,
Thompson, David, *Nevada Events 1776-1985*, Reno: Grace Danberg Foundation, 1987
Townley, John M., *Tough Little Town on the Truckee*, Reno: Jamison Station Press, 1983
Williams III, George, *Mark Twain, His Life in Virginia City, Nevada*, Riverside: Tree By the River Publishing, 1985
—*Mark Twain, His Adventures At Aurora and Mono Lake*, Riverside: Tree By the River Publishing, 1985
—*Mark Twain, Jackass Hill and the Jumping Frog*, Riverside: Tree By the River Publishing, 1985
Wilson, Thomas, *Pioneer Nevada, Reno: Harold's Club, 1951*
—*Pioneer Nevada, Vol. 2, Reno: Harold's Club, 1956*